THRIVING ON COLLABORATIVE GENIUS

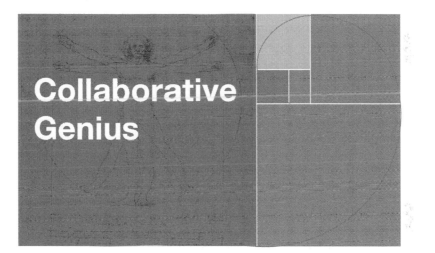

Collaborative Genius

The *Art* of
Bringing Organizations
to *Life*

James Graham Johnston

mse
PRESS

Cover design by Julie Lee

The cover includes an image of a spiral galaxy from ESA/Hubble and an image of Leonardo da Vinci's drawing, "Vitruvian Man," housed in Gallerie dell'Accademia, Venice. The spiral line and progressive rectilinear grid on the cover depict the "golden mean" accredited to Pythagoras and applied in Aristotle's ethics as a middle way that reconciles extremes. Spiral galaxies, da Vinci's "Mona Lisa," and many natural forms are also considered representations of the golden mean.

Thriving on Collaborative Genius

ISBN: 1-4499-8072-4

ISBN-13: 978-1449980726

Library of Congress Control Number: 2010901754

For correspondence or permissions, please contact: info@partnersfi.com

Perrysburg, Ohio

Contents

About Partners for Innovation ix
Acknowledgments xi
Introduction xiii

Leadership 1

Managing the New Knowledge Workers 3

How to Liberate Creativity 5

Leadership and Collaborative Genius 8

Any Road Could Take You There 11

Pursue the Light of Success 13

Convey a Mission that Matters 15

Compassion: The Heart of Leadership 17

Humility and an Iron Will 19

The Tao of Dialogue 21

Character: The Keystone of Leadership 23

Bringing the Soul to Life: The Leader's Role 25

The Power of Shared Leadership 27

Quality Decisions: The Productive Advantage 29

Listen, *Then* Change 31

Cultivate Individuals, Not Tactics 33

Manage as if You Had No Power 35

Learn to Play Well with Others 37

The New *Feminine* Leadership 39

Leadership: Follow Through 41

Social Architecture 43

The New Realities: The Great Divide 45

The One Right Structure 47

Learning from the Chicago Bulls 49

Productivity in the New Economy 51

Building Innovation into the Organization's DNA 53

The New Organizational Chart 55

Boards as Strategic Collaborators 57

Order Versus Control: Geese or Pyramids? 59

The Donut of Evolutionary Change 61

The Way of the Herd or of the Individual? 64

It Takes a Village 66

Social Architecture: Follow Through 68

Social Capital 71

BHAGS: The Catalytic Goals of Great Groups 73

Why Can't They Be Like We Were? 75

Dialogue or Discussion? 77

Suspending Judgment: The Threshold to Dialogue 79

Diversity: The Innovative Difference 81

Dissent: The Key Catalyst for Innovation 83

Changing the Soul and Energy of a Company 85

Ebenezer Scrooge and the Path to Possibility 87

Christmas Compassion 89

The Essential Attributes of Great Groups 91

Fire in the Belly 93

In Hot Pursuit of Fire in the Belly 95

Duplicity: The Saboteur of Collaboration 98

Social Capital: The Rising Tide for All Boats 100

The Triple Spiral of Social Capital 103

The Vital Flow of Face-to-Face Meetings 105

People as Partners 107

The Call to Inquiry and Ingenuity 109

Hire for Attitude 111

The 360 Degree Preview 113

The Extreme Makeover Job Description 115

Having Fun at Work: Work Like a Dog 117

Go With the Flow 119

Strengthen the Core 121

The Question: "Who?" 124

Do You Have a Teeming V Organization? 126

Building Forces for Good to Great 128

Social Capital: Follow Through 131

Soul 133

Soul: Keep it Alive 135

The Archetypal Self: Vivifying Cooperation 137

Rooting Our Work in the Dream of God 139

Soul and Collaborative Genius 141

The Soul Aroused 144

The Collective Dream 147

Enthusiasm and the Implicit Order 149

Values First, Profits Second 151

Dialogue: The Heart of Community 153

Bringing the Soul to Life: Liberating Creativity 155

Trust the Undercurrent of Change 159

Heart 161

Self Actualization 163

A Life of Quality 165

Soul: Follow Through 168

Innovation 171

The Mission: Innovating for a Purpose 173

Seizing Opportunity: Unexpected Success 175

Getting Innovations Accepted 177

Solving the Problem or *My* Solution? 179

Complaints: The Wellspring of Innovation 181

Basic Elements of Successful Innovation 183

The Discipline of Innovation 185

Disruptive Innovation 187

Understanding the Starting Point 189

Strategic Planning or Strategic Innovation? 191

Implicit Rules: the "Hobgoblin" of Innovation 193

Paying Attention in the Age of Discontinuity 195

Organized Abandonment: Unplugging the TV 197

Abandon: But When? 199

Testing Prototypes: Not Betting the Farm 202

The Flywheel of Innovation 204

The Hedgehog or the Fox? 206

"What If?": The Catalytic Question 209

Expect the Unexpected 211

Relentless Reflection 213

Implement Quickly 215

Intuition 217

Catalytic Learning 219

Suspending Bias 221

Incongruities: A Potent Window of Opportunity 223

Failure: The Great Learning Experience 225

Slow Cook the Big Innovations 227

The Free Flow of Informal Conversation 229

Adaptive Learning 231

The Three Strokes of Effective Innovation 233

The Flower of Strategic Innovation 236

Innovation: Follow Through 239

Further Reading 241

About the Author 253

About Partners for Innovation

Partners for Innovation, Inc. was founded to train and coach people to thrive on their own collaborative genius. The founders synthesized their experience with art, architecture, business, Jungian psychology, religion, sociology, and organizational development to develop a few core methodologies for collaborative innovation. The scope of those methodologies could be summarized by a simple maxim for effective innovation: *Learn, Talk, & Create.*

Learn

Our *Seven Sources Inventory*™ is a means of assessing opportunities for operational or strategic change.

Talk

Our workshops on Reflective and Generative Dialogue help to prepare people for collaborative innovation. We use the *GifsCompass*™ *Inventory* (www.GiftsCompass.com) in these workshops to alert people to their highest potential contributions.

Create

Inspired by migratory geese and their V-shaped formation, our *Teeming V*™ *Dialogue* enables people to swiftly and systematically develop highly creative solutions to complex problems, *together.*

For more information, please visit: www.partnersfi.com. To register for free email essays, like those included in this book, please click on "Innovation Tips" at the web site.

Acknowledgements

None of these essays would have been possible without the productive efforts of Partners for Innovation staff who worked fruitfully and often tirelessly to produce excellent service for our varied clients. Many of the insights included in this book were born from the collaborative experience of delivering our services.

The associates who have helped to deliver the work of Partners for Innovation include: Tesse Akpeki, Curtis Clark, Linda DeArment, Joycelyn Degener, Barbara Eikost, William Glover, Lynn Kampfer, James Latimer, Michelle Mesker, Marvin Moore, Karin Rade, Margie Spino, Angelo Spoto, Chris Stearns, and Karen Steiner. (Individual contributions to the following essays are noted at the end of an essay.)

Barbara Eikost deserves special acknowledgement for without her exuberant enthusiasm, encouragement, and supreme confidence neither the company nor these essays would have ever been born.

Angelo Spoto and Marvin Moore, my co-founders of Partners for Innovation, also deserve special acknowledgement for their patient and dedicated work in helping to formulate the methodologies that would uniquely distinguish Partners for Innovation.

JGJ

Introduction

This book, *Thriving on Collaborative Genius*, has been compiled from ten years of essays called, "Innovation Tips." The essays have been written and distributed regularly as a service to our clients. They are the outcome of our research, hands-on experience in organizations, and dialogue among staff. Together, they provide some of our best advice on how to "thrive on collaborative genius." The essays have been organized by five themes:

Leadership
We begin with the theme of leadership for organizations do not engage their highest potential unless leaders enable it.

Social Architecture
If the social architecture is not well designed, it can do more to impede collaboration than to support it.

Social Capital
Without strong social capital, collaboration does not occur.

Soul
The "over-world" of soul constitutes the vital infrastructure for fruitful human endeavor.

Innovation
Innovation is the very purpose of our work and an indispensable element of collaborative genius.

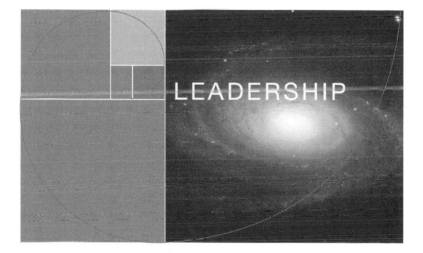

LEADERSHIP

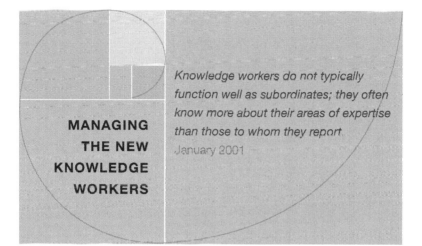

MANAGING THE NEW KNOWLEDGE WORKERS

Knowledge workers do not typically function well as subordinates; they often know more about their areas of expertise than those to whom they report

January 2001

With innovation, what we *unlearn* is sometimes as important as what we learn. The paradigms, the processes, the implicit rules that proved successful in the past must sometimes be abandoned to make way for a new and more successful way of operating.

As Peter Drucker makes clear in his book, *Management Challenges for the 21st Century*, organizations now need new and innovative approaches to *management*. People in the work force, whether in for-profit or non-profit organizations, are increasingly becoming *knowledge workers*—people who come to the organization with highly developed core competencies based in *knowledge* rather than manual skills.

Knowledge workers do not typically function well as subordinates; they often know more about their areas of expertise than those to whom they report. It makes little sense for them to take orders from a boss in a command-and-control environment. More important is the need to integrate and share their knowledge and experience to enhance the viability of the organization.

This is the emerging challenge: how to "manage" very independent people with highly specialized knowledge.

Models are only just beginning to emerge to capture that increasingly complex task. For Margaret Wheatley (management consultant and author of *A Simpler Way*) and Arie De Geus (former planner with Royal Dutch Shell and author of *The Living Company*), the metaphors are drawn from organic life suggesting a flow of information that is dynamic and evolving. Drucker imagines a symphony conductor where the manager only leads and provides focus—that is, *orchestrates* the various participants.

On this key point, each of these emerging models agrees: knowledge workers need to be liberated to be creative and responsive. Theirs is not a submissive role but a proactive one. The ideal environment is one that cultivates what Abraham Maslow called *self-actualization* where people are passionately engaged in using their knowledge to do work they consider to be important.

How do you manage people who know more than you about their work and need to be passionately and creatively engaged in it? Discover new ways to liberate their work, not control it.

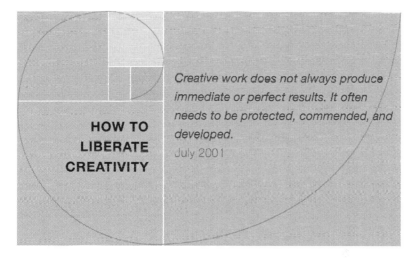

Creative work does not always produce immediate or perfect results. It often needs to be protected, commended, and developed.

July 2001

Techniques for killing creativity are easy and pervasive. We may all have a tendency to apply them without thinking. In her article, "How to Kill Creativity" (*Harvard Business Review*), Teresa Amabile identified a few of the many destructive habits in organizations that suppress, rather than stimulate, creativity. Her list may look all too familiar:

1. Undermine Autonomy

Change goals and interfere with the work processes of others.

2. Mismanage Resources

Put teams under artificial constraints of time or resources.

3. Be Critical

Routinely criticize new suggestions; thoroughly assess each new idea for its flaws.

4. Be Secretive

Create an atmosphere of mistrust.

5. Analyze Too Much
Analyze the life out of every proposition.

6. Let Politics Prevail
Allow internal politics to take precedence over evaluating ideas on their own merits.

These techniques may seem familiar because they are too often practiced, either consciously or inadvertently. They are vestigial remnants of outmoded management practices. We must vigilantly avoid them if we are to cultivate creative thinking.

Amabile also identified important conditions for creating a healthy context for creative thinking. These are among the principles that will cultivate vitality and enable the collaborative genius of an organization to thrive.

1. Build Competence
People need to be highly competent in their areas of specialized knowledge.

2. Affirm Creative Thinking
Creative thinking needs to become a way of life in the organization. Affirm creative thinking as an integral element of the organization's culture.

3. Provide Extrinsic Motivation
The intrinsic desire to be creative ought to be coupled with incentives that reward creative thinking.

4. Sculpt Teams Around Gifts
Sculpt the work of individuals to optimize their best gifts. Create diverse interdependent teams of people with complementary gifts.

5. Honor Autonomy

Give people freedom to respond to the needs of the work within the context of core values.

6. Allocate Sufficient Resources

Creating something on a shoestring does exercise the creative juices, but it also tends to focus that creative thinking on saving resources rather than on solving the problem at hand. Allocate sufficient resources to enable people to keep their focus on the project.

7. Acknowledge Creative Work

Creative work does not always produce immediate or perfect results. It often needs to be protected, commended, and developed. Part of the leader's role is to be sure that everyone understands that creative work is valued for its own sake, as well as for what it produces.

We live in an age of increasing change and challenge. To thrive in this new age, we must learn to cultivate creative thinking in the work place—to thrive on collaborative genius and innovation. Following these few principles can help to accelerate innovative thinking and boost the performance of the whole organization.

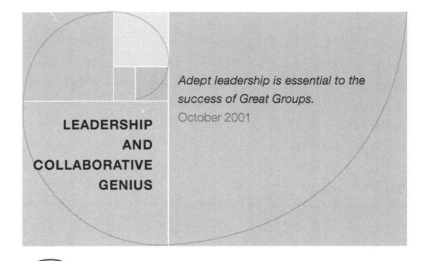

LEADERSHIP AND COLLABORATIVE GENIUS

Adept leadership is essential to the success of Great Groups.

October 2001

G*reat Groups* occur where collaborative genius thrives and collaborative genius thrives where leadership is adept. Lao Tse's adage that the best leaders will leave people feeling as if they did it themselves applies here. The leaders who orchestrate Great Groups do so by bringing the best out of those doing the work—not by telling them what to do.

This form of leadership is more art than science and bears careful examination. Great Groups across various industries, from Lockheed's Skunk Works, to the Disney team that produced *Snow White*, to the Orpheus Chamber Orchestra give us clues about the art of leading Great Groups. At least seven attributes of leadership seem to be consistently present among those who effectively orchestrate Great Groups:

1. They inspire the loyalty of their coworkers.

They often possess solid integrity and will fiercely defend the well-being of their groups against disruptive influences.

2. They are passionate about the work.

They are often the most enthusiastically committed people on the team.

3. They are navigate the flow of ideas and talent.

These leaders do not micromanage or create a lot of rules; they orchestrate, facilitate, and cross-pollinate. They let the passion inherent in these groups emerge and flourish. They find ways for people to apply their energy where they are most gifted.

4. They are adept at drawing out the best in others.

People readily give their best to these groups and often feel challenged to deliver 110%. These leaders typically gather the best talent they can find and then remind them of their exceptional abilities. They raise the bar of performance and encourage the group to take on outlandish goals.

5. They are collaborative.

They seldom make big decisions without involving others, especially those who might be affected by the decision. The bigger the decision, the more people they will often involve. They rely on the insights and perspectives of their coworkers to develop key decisions and to build consensus.

6. They carry a vision of the whole.

They often carry a complete mental picture of the work of the whole enterprise and they know how the work of every individual relates to it.

7. They are attentive to the value of each individual.

Each member of the group, regardless of role, understands that his role is significant and valued.

Adept leadership is essential to the success of Great Groups. Sometimes that leadership is shared or rotated through the group; sometimes one individual serves as the primary leader. Either way, simple principles of leadership apply: facilitate rather than manage; convey a vision of the whole; engender trust; elicit the best from each member of the group; and, perhaps most importantly, let your own passion and enthusiasm for the work flourish.

In our constantly changing, global, highly technological society, collaboration is a necessity. The Lone Ranger, the incarnation of the individual problem-solver, is dead. In his place, we have a new model for creative achievement: the Great Group.

Warren Bennis and Patricia Biederman

Organizing Genius

ANY ROAD COULD TAKE YOU THERE

It is certainly important for everyone to understand the purpose of the organization—to understand its fundamental mission. But it is not so important to have rigidly defined strategies for attaining that mission.

January 2002

W*hen you don't know where you are going, any road will take you there.* We may have read that humorous Cheshire-cat aphorism before and thought, "The absence of planning, what folly! A recipe for disaster."

The traditional approach says we must have a plan; we must know what road to take to get to our destination. It must be budgeted and defined and well thought out in advance. The success of an organizational leader is defined by his ability to articulate a direction and then stick to it. And there certainly is something to be said for planning and having a firm direction.

Yet, a rigid direction also has a way of snuffing out dynamic opportunities. The organization that has fixed, unyielding strategies can be too narrowly focused. People can miss the serendipitous and unexpected opportunities that may lie just outside the strategies.

Paradoxically, organizations can sometimes arrive at a destination more successfully if the leadership does *not* know exactly how to get there or precisely which road to be on.

The any-road-could-take-you-there approach alluded to in the above aphorism, elicits a more feminine, intently responsive approach that can more readily recognize unexpected opportunities, ideas, and insights.

This may sound improbable, but let's think about it. Creative ideas can flourish amidst uncertainty. When people are not completely reliant on a manager for their marching orders, they have a tacit opening to take the initiative themselves.

Strategies that are too well defined can stifle the creative ideas of the people doing the work. People can become too focused, like drones, on getting the work out, rather than on innovating to more effectively achieve the organization's purposes.

If people feel that a leader is unequivocally certain about process and strategy, they will be less likely to contribute ideas that are outside the norm. Yet that is precisely where the best ideas come from.

Uncertainty can also promote greater egalitarianism. If a leader is uncertain and willing to entertain the certainty of others, the door is opened for others to voice their ideas and their perspectives.

It is certainly important for everyone to understand the purpose of the organization—to understand its fundamental mission—but it is not as important to have rigidly defined strategies for attaining that mission. Better to let the purpose serve as a guiding compass that engenders potential strategies and ideas for attaining the mission.

When you engage people in generating ideas, projects, and strategies to achieve the purposes of the organization, many of *their* roads could take you there.

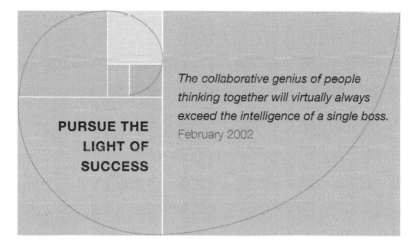

PURSUE THE
LIGHT OF
SUCCESS

The collaborative genius of people thinking together will virtually always exceed the intelligence of a single boss.
February 2002

Managers are apt to be problem solvers. They are expected to make the executive judgments that fix problems. Yet, they can be more effective as leaders if they would share the pain of problem solving with others. To lead, their time would be better spent pursuing the light of success.

Managers serve more as leaders when they let others fix problems and encourage people to move in the direction of common dreams, purposes, and especially success. The Pareto 80/20 rule offers apt counsel: leaders could aspire to spend 80% of their time praising, encouraging, recognizing, and identifying successes, and 20% of their time solving problems.

People who are doing the work, who are most affected by a problem, are almost always better equipped to bring a successful solution to a problem. The collaborative genius of people thinking together will virtually always exceed the intelligence of a single boss.

When people are engaged in solving their own operational problems, they take deeper ownership for the work; they experience the satisfaction of achievement. Taking orders from a problem-solving boss numbs initiative and suppresses creative problem solving.

A leader can often better accomplish the purposes of an organization by observing where the organization is having its greatest successes, and navigating the movement of the enterprise toward those successes. The leader's key role is to pursue the light of success—to encourage, promote, commend, acknowledge, and pursue success at every turn.

Many of the great organizational success stories have been born of pursuing unexpected success. The multibillion-dollar international McDonald's corporation was born when salesman Ray Kroc noticed that a small hamburger shop in California was buying an unusual number of milkshake blenders.

Honda Motor Corporation captured the majority of the U.S. motorcycle market by noticing public interest in three employees who were using their Super Cub motorbikes for weekend recreation.

Chrysler made windfall profits on the LeBaron convertible when Lee Iacocca noticed that a lot of people were asking him about the prototype he was driving around town.

The acclaimed management thinker, Peter Drucker, has observed that the easiest, most accessible, most fruitful innovations in any industry are often born from *unexpected* success. It is the leader's role to notice success when it occurs and build on it—to let these successes guide the organization's growth and development.

In the same way that plants turn toward light, leaders can turn their organizations toward the same light of success that has guided many organizations to abundant prosperity.

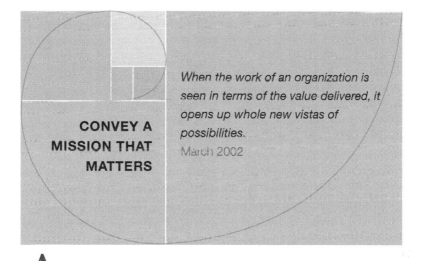

CONVEY A MISSION THAT MATTERS

When the work of an organization is seen in terms of the value delivered, it opens up whole new vistas of possibilities.

March 2002

Abraham Maslow once noted that the only happy people he knew were the ones working well at something they considered important. All of his "self-actualized" clients had one thing in common—they were motivated by some great and important job. As Matthew Fox noted, "We all want to be part of something big and sacred."

But most organizations do not look at the big and sacred side of what they do; they stick to the prosaic. They usually define their mission in terms of products or services rather than in terms of the value they deliver to others. Conveying a mission in terms of products and services rather than value delivered creates two key problems:

1. People become oblivious to opportunities for *innovation*.

2. People feel less *committed* to the mission of the organization.

Innovation

Think of the oft-cited buggy whip manufacturers of the turn of the century. They likely thought they were in the business of making buggy whips, and they went out of business when the need for buggy whips evaporated.

People only bought buggy whips because they wanted *mobility*. If the manufacturers had seen their work from the standpoint of the value delivered to their constituency—mobility—they would have been more attentive to the technological changes in progress; they could have more readily seen the available windows of opportunity.

When the whole organization is aware of the value delivered to a customer or constituency, everyone in the organization can be mindful of opportunities to fulfill that value.

Commitment

What is the value delivered to others? That is the mission, the great and important job, the one we may begin to see as big and sacred. Insurance companies deliver peace of mind to their clients; they issue policies only as a means to that end. Hospitals comfort and heal the infirm; their medical equipment and services are only the means to that end.

When people begin to get a sense of the larger purpose of their work, the one that affects the lives of others in meaningful and fruitful ways, they bring a different level of commitment to their work. They can approach their work, like Maslow's clients, feeling that they are doing something significant with their lives.

Seeing work in terms of the *value delivered* opens up new vistas of innovative possibilities. The culture of the organization changes; camaraderie and initiative gain momentum.

COMPASSION: THE HEART OF LEADERSHIP

Those leaders who have the empathy to take a compassionate and nonjudgmental interest in others establish a rapport that engenders good will, relaxed communication, and creative dialogue.
May 2002

What quality ensures peoples' loyalty to a leader? The leader's intelligence, wit, talent, bravado, and knowledge may certainly all contribute, but one attribute must also be present for that loyalty to be compelling: *compassion*.

It has been said that people don't really care how much you know; they want to know how much you care. The dispassionate leader—however bold, talented, intelligent, or witty—may gain the admiration of others but will fail to gain compelling loyalty. Perhaps only compassion holds that power.

Compassion has been the centerpiece of the world's most profound religious thinkers for millennia. From the Hebrew prophets to Buddha to Jesus, compassion is at the heart of the way of life commended by the great teachers.

Yet compassion at work often takes a back seat to egotism, prestige, and pride. Leaders may become more intent on developing a commanding persona than on developing an authentic interest in others.

The word *compassion* comes from the Greek roots meaning "to come alongside another's feelings or suffering." It requires seeing life from another's perspective—to understand, respond and honor another's history and viewpoint.

Those leaders who have the empathy to take a compassionate and nonjudgmental interest in others establish a rapport that engenders good will, relaxed communication, and creative dialogue.

Few people ever let their guards down around people who judge them. Judgment of others is perhaps the most frequent obstacle to a compassionate life. We all judge, every day; judgment is an automatic faculty built into us, like breathing. Attaining compassion is often a matter of being bigger than the judgment—of being *kind* rather than *right*.

Criticism, self-righteousness, and judgment are easy—just as destroying a great work of art is much easier than creating it or cutting down a fruit-bearing tree is easier than growing it.

Cultivating and developing compassion and nonjudgmental acceptance are difficult, but they are worth the effort. They bear the fruit of an artful and graceful way of life. For leaders, they bear the added fruit of generating a resilient bond of loyalty. People who work with a compassionate leader know that they are valued—and that makes all the difference.

The compassionate leader, in learning to value others, takes a quantum leap into a mode of leadership that engenders uncommon commitment. Those leaders who are most effective at developing collaborative genius, like the ancient religious teachers, transcend judgment with compassion. They are big enough to be kind rather than right.

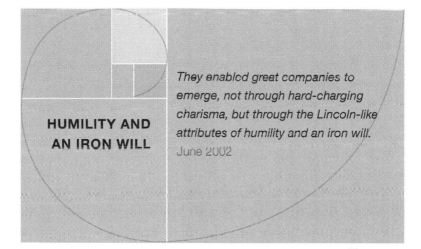

They enabled great companies to emerge, not through hard-charging charisma, but through the Lincoln-like attributes of humility and an iron will.
June 2002

HUMILITY AND AN IRON WILL

Who comes to mind when you think of effective leaders? In business, those who gain the most attention—the more charismatic and conspicuous executives gracing the covers of business periodicals—tend to be the ones we think of first. But recent research suggests considering a different model, one closer to the attributes of Abraham Lincoln: leaders who possess humility and an iron will.

From exhaustive research for their recently published book, *Good to Great*, Jim Collins and a team of researchers noticed a striking anomaly among the companies they studied. In the companies that had successfully transitioned from mediocre to astonishingly successful, the leaders were *not* illustrious.

The chief executives in these companies were *not* among those frequently interviewed by the prominent business journals. Their names were scarcely recognizable—Darwin Smith, Colman Mockler, David Maxwell, George Cain and other unknowns. These leaders were more intent on building the living architecture of an enduring enterprise than building their own name recognition.

They were humble, often self-effacing, yet firmly committed to the central purposes of their organizations.

They gathered bright, highly talented people around them and had the humility to give those people largely free reign. These leaders held to the organizational purpose, once they discerned it, with an iron will. Like Lincoln, they could be humble and self-effacing, but—also like Lincoln—they were unyielding about the purpose of the work.

But companies must aspire to the kinds of financial returns for which Lee Iacocca, Jack Welch and others are famous. And that's the rub. The companies Collins studied produced *better* financial returns than the G.E.s and Chryslers of the world, and often outperformed them by a wide margin.

Companies in rather unspectacular industries like groceries, steel, and consumer products attained spectacular rates of return and outperformed the stars that were drawing most of the media attention. All the companies in the study generated rates of financial return that were three to eighteen times greater than the stock market as a whole.

These leaders cultivated the collaborative genius of people as they built enduring organizational cultures. They enabled great companies to emerge, not through hard-charging charisma, but through the Lincoln-like attributes *of humility and an iron will.*

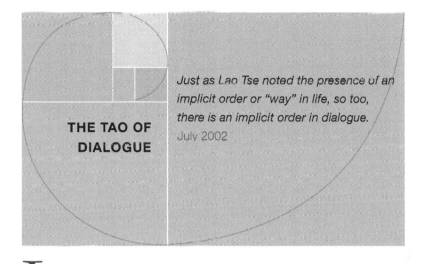

THE TAO OF DIALOGUE

Just as Lao Tse noted the presence of an implicit order or "way" in life, so too, there is an implicit order in dialogue.
July 2002

Lao Tse, the sixth century B.C. sage whose religious philosophy of Taoism has thrived for over two millennia, spoke reverently of the *Tao*—a divine way, an order implicit in all life. But the Tao is not easily grasped. Of the Tao, Lao Tse is reported to have said, "He who knows, does not say; and he who says, does not know."

Just as Lao Tse perceived an implicit order, so too there is an implicit order in dialogue.

Leadership, in highly collaborative and creative dialogue, does not come from the leader. It emerges from within the group, from the underlying Tao of dialogue. Truly generative dialogue permits what Carl Jung used to call a "third way not given" to emerge amid opposing views—a way that both rises above and resolves conflict.

It is a way that no one may control or dictate; it can only be observed. The leader who says he leads the group in this dialogue simply "does not know." The most important contribution a leader can make to such dialogue is to avoid controlling the group.

The leader must not impose his will or order on the flow of dialogue, for the flow of dialogue has its own order, its own destination, and its own resolution. The leader's primary role is to ensure that everyone's views are equitably heard. Everyone's views must be listened to with the same level of respect and attention. No one may have a "more equal" voice than anyone else—not even the leader—or the expression of the Tao will be suppressed.

Few groups ever experience the Tao of dialogue; people attending to their persona, their political position, or their self-interest will keep the group boxed in. Only when each member of a group is authentically committed to the welfare of the group's purpose above his own may the Tao of dialogue fully emerge to guide the group on its collective path.

Leaders who are skilled in cultivating collaborative genius know that the Tao offers greater leadership than they could ever hope to provide. They have only to arrange the context for this implicit order to arrive—and arrive it does. But as to how or why, those who have known the Tao "can't say."

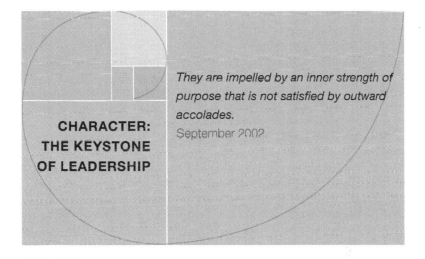

CHARACTER:
THE KEYSTONE
OF LEADERSHIP

They are impelled by an inner strength of purpose that is not satisfied by outward accolades.

September 2002

W e have reviewed some of the attributes of leadership that are essential for the development of collaborative genius. We have looked at the Tao of dialogue, humility and an iron will, compassion, shared leadership, following the light of success, and being clear about purpose but flexible about means. Yet, there is one more attribute that must be added, like a keystone in an arch, lest the others collapse. That attribute is *character*.

It was said, long ago, that he who rules himself is greater than he who rules a city. That statement could have come from any one of many ancient sages, for it is consistent with highly regarded teachers from Socrates and Plato to Confucius and Lao Tse.

The struggle that leads from egocentricity to character is the universal human struggle. It transcends all boundaries of time, place, and culture. Each person must confront that struggle—the "hero's journey" to the center of the soul. Those who make that inward journey and return with the capacity to "rule themselves" are those who are most adept at engaging collaborative genius.

They become authentic, and authenticity breeds trust and collaboration.

Authenticity makes all things easier. It frees up life and enables change. Those who have found the authenticity of the inner life, who have engaged in and even relish the struggle with egocentricity, are willing to sustain any change. They are often eager to explore the next episode in life that may lead to their even more substantial character.

They have achieved an apogee of inner success that is greater than "he who rules a city." They are the ones who can deftly navigate collaborative innovation, for they need no credit. They are open to change and opportunity; they encourage and acknowledge the achievements of others. Disappointments spur them on and challenges invigorate them. They are impelled by an inner strength of purpose that is not satisfied by outward accolades.

They have character. Without that keystone the arch of creative collaboration does not stand.

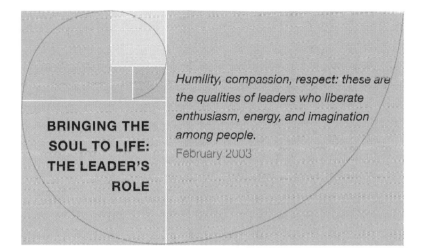

BRINGING THE SOUL TO LIFE: THE LEADER'S ROLE

Humility, compassion, respect: these are the qualities of leaders who liberate enthusiasm, energy, and imagination among people.

February 2003

I n organizations where the soul is alive and well, the leadership is different. Leaders in these organizations engender compassion, listening, and collaboration.

Leaders who listen, who respect the value of individuals, who encourage dialogue and collaboration, who keep the common good uppermost, bring the entire organization to life.

They engender a livelier, more organic, and responsive order. They create the context for people to take risks, to push the envelope of opportunity, and to bring enthusiasm to their work.

Imagination, energy, enthusiasm, fun, passion, and dialogue: these are all qualities of soul. The leader intent on delivering these qualities attends to the well-being of the people in the organization and becomes more focused on serving than on being served.

Authoritarian leaders, by contrast, are bent on control and on protecting their position as top dog. Their style promotes a competitive culture—a "zero-sum game"—where one person's gain is another person's loss. Their autocratic style suppresses collaboration. Instead of collaborative dialogue, people become increasingly focused on protecting their turf, on looking good for the boss, or on vying for positions of influence.

Autocratic leaders make trouble for the whole organization by confusing control with order. Their control produces an immature, rigid organizational structure that disables the richer, more complex, and fluid order of people freely collaborating toward a common purpose.

Control-oriented leaders stifle the collective soul. Their work tends to be less about the success of the people in the organization and more about their own power or prestige. They can be self-serving rather than serving the common good of the organization and the people in it

Humility, compassion, and respect: these are qualities of leaders who liberate enthusiasm, energy, and imagination among people. They are qualities too infrequently acknowledged, admired, advocated, or attained. But when they are attained, the soul of an organization comes to life.

———

THE POWER OF SHARED LEADERSHIP

They create clear roles while they share and rotate leadership. They have learned to really listen and to talk together in a way that generates consensus and productive outcomes.

April 2004

The Orpheus Chamber Orchestra has been described as one of the great marvels of the music world. They have been thrilling music lovers on four continents for 31 years.

Orpheus has changed the way people think about musicians and their roles in orchestras, for they perform *without* a conductor. The musicians have mastered the art of *shared leadership*. Their unique approach, the "Orpheus Process," has been the subject of two documentary films, a book, and numerous articles.

Orpheus puts control in the hands of the people doing the work. They create clear roles while they share and rotate leadership. They have learned to really listen and to talk together in a way that generates consensus and productive outcomes. Few organizations of any type have attained their acumen for creative collaboration.

To achieve their success, they have broken some centuries-old customs. Orchestras have traditionally followed the command-and-control model of organizational leadership: The conductor decides and the musicians conform. Consequently, the job satisfaction among traditional musicians has sometimes plummeted to levels reported by prison guards.

The job satisfaction among Orpheus musicians is at the top of the charts. Their musicians have a voice in what and how music is performed. They develop a spirited consensus through collaborative dialogue.

What the Orpheus musicians do in performing music, people in other organizations could also do in the way they work together. The orchestra's non-hierarchical decision-making style engenders strong commitment and highly collaborative outcomes. They have a long waiting list of musicians aspiring to get into their orchestra.

Would you also like to have people queued up to join your organization? Consider the Orpheus approach to *shared leadership*.

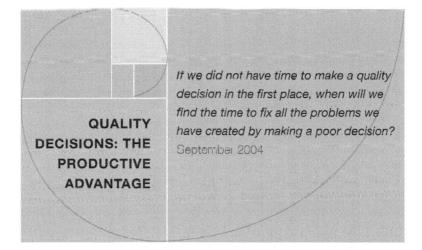

QUALITY DECISIONS: THE PRODUCTIVE ADVANTAGE

If we did not have time to make a quality decision in the first place, when will we find the time to fix all the problems we have created by making a poor decision?
September 2004

Our culture exalts expediency. We are driven to make a decision and implement it. We are surrounded by an increasing array of timesaving and laborsaving gadgets and machines. We get more done in a day, send more messages, have more phone conversations, and accomplish more tasks than ever before in modern history. Yet to what end?

Most of us feel frenetic and worn thin. The timesaving gadgets have only given us more to do. We have not more available time, but less. We are not settled, but caught up in the daily swirl of endless activity.

Make the sale, complete the task, do the job, implement the project. In the frenzy of activity, we have lost the patience to take time to think through our decisions. Instead, we shoot from the hip and think that we have accomplished something grand because we have made the decision in record time.

Yet, decisions made in haste will often create more problems than they solve. If we did not have time to make a quality decision in the first place, when will we find the time to fix all the problems we have created by making a poor decision?

The key to growing productivity in organizations is not speed but quality. W. Edwards Deming preached quality to managers in America after World War II. Few listened, but Japanese industrialists heard him and gradually created some of the most productive companies and reliable products in the world. They succeeded by following Deming's advice: *they took time to make quality decisions.*

Decisions of high quality are generated by *systems thinking*—decisions made through dialogue among people affected by the outcomes. Japanese companies developed a reputation for extraordinary quality, in part by letting people doing the work make the decisions about how best to do that work.

It seems so simple, yet it is so uncommon. Few organizations actually operate that way. We tend instead to get entangled in egocentric agendas and political hierarchies, exalting speed, volume, and prestige over quality and humility.

Quick decisions from the top contribute little enduring value to the social capital of the organization. They build no sense of ownership; they generate resentment from those left out; and they fail to engender collective enthusiasm. Though the "boss" may feel powerful, decisive, and strong, too often these single-minded decisions are simply decisive and *wrong.*

Quality decision-making requires patience and tolerance for diverse perspectives. Like the postwar Japanese companies, organizations where people are taking time for quality decision-making will also likely enjoy phenomenal economic productivity. In this age of expediency, not more haste but more *patience* will win the day.

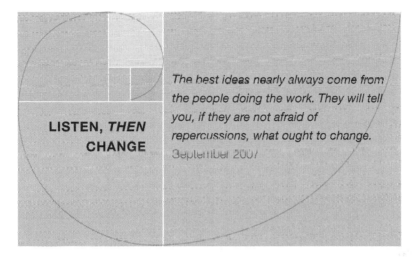

LISTEN, *THEN* CHANGE

The best ideas nearly always come from the people doing the work. They will tell you, if they are not afraid of repercussions, what ought to change.

September 2007

W e have said that organizations become vital and endure to the degree that the people who join them are respected, encouraged, and valued *individually.*

Who really does that? Our experience and research suggest that very few organizations promote the value of unique individuals. Most rely on chain-of-command models of reward and punishment that build a homogeneous *work force.*

They are highly organized and tightly controlled, harnessing strength in numbers, alignment with mission, vision, and values, corporate loyalty, and clear lines of responsibility. Wow! A CEO's dream.

But an individual's nightmare.

For individuals to be fully valued, their dreams, their individual missions, visions, and values, their ideas, and their divergence from common agreement must be trusted and respected.

If leaders are to truly tap the full potential of the people in their organizations, they have to create the organization that is the dream for the *individual,* not for the CEO.

This would constitute an enormous shift in leadership for many. For some, it would be unthinkable and frightening. But here is a simple way to find out if this sort of shift could work in your organization.

Ask.

Just ask the people who work there what the ideal culture would look like, if they could create the organization anew. What would they change about the way things are done, if they could do it any way they chose?

Then listen.

The best ideas nearly always come from the people doing the work. They'll tell you, if they are not afraid of repercussions, what ought to change.

Then change it.

Look to the successful organizations and you will find people willing to fail, freely sharing ideas, taking risks, and venturing out into uncertain territory.
July/August 2007

Align with the vision; drive the results; meet the goals; attain the objectives; set the strategies; create the plan; carry out the tactics; deliver results. Are we building organizations or invading Iraq?

The common wisdom about managing organizations suggests that we can operate them like tanks: blow the competition away; win customers; capture market share.

Enough already. How many organizations built on the military model have to fall before we get the message: *Do not* manage people like troops; the CEO is *not* a Commander in Chief.

Yes, organizations are formed to deliver some particular mission. No, we do not have to manage the people in them like faceless armies to successfully deliver that value. Organizations are not nation states and they are not at war.

Vital, successful, enduring organizations have learned to cultivate *individuals*. The people who lead them humbly acknowledge the value of others. It is not much more difficult than that.

Look to the really successful organizational cultures in any arena and you will find people everywhere in the organization being cultivated for their individual value. Look to the lackluster organizations and you will find people being used as pawns to accomplish objectives, strategies, and tactics.

Look to the successful organizations and you will find people willing to fail, freely sharing ideas, taking risks, and venturing out into uncertain territory.

Look to the mediocre organizations and you will find people entrenched, defending their positions, protecting their jobs, blindly pursuing narrow objectives, making their "unit" look good, and ostracizing dissenters.

How many cultures that promote the value of individuals have to succeed beyond anyone's imagination before we understand the premise that prevails in them? They are built on *uncommon* common sense: organizations become vital and endure when the people who join them are respected, encouraged, and valued individually.

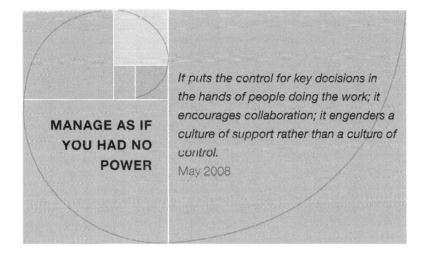

MANAGE AS IF YOU HAD NO POWER

It puts the control for key decisions in the hands of people doing the work; it encourages collaboration; it engenders a culture of support rather than a culture of control.

May 2008

In 1968, when Rene McPherson was named President of Dana Corporation, one of his first innovations was to throw out the 22 ½-inch-thick policy manuals and replace them with a one-page statement of principles.

With his relaxed and friendly leadership style, McPherson inaugurated a new culture at Dana that emphasized collaboration and an absence of control from the top. The whole company changed; operations became leaner, morale grew stronger, people everywhere in the company took greater responsibility for quality and productivity.

After a decade of McPherson's leadership, the company was among the few featured in the best-selling business book—*In Search of Excellence.*

But the culture he established eventually eroded. Control from the top gradually resumed; management launched forays into unfamiliar industries; the values and principles he advocated lost their appeal.

To the shock and surprise of an admiring public, by 2006, Dana Corporation was bankrupt.

In 2008, after stockholders lost their entire investment in the company, Dana emerged from Chapter 11 reorganization. A new CEO, Gary Convis, was hired. From his extensive experience as head of Toyota's North American manufacturing operations, Convis began promoting a management philosophy that could have been spoken by McPherson:

"Manage as if you have no power."

That simple management principle will transform a culture the way that McPherson transformed Dana in the 1970's. It puts the control for key decisions in the hands of people doing the work; it encourages collaboration; it engenders a culture of support rather than a culture of control.

It will once again transform Dana.

The beauty of that simple principle is that it implicitly creates collaborative teams. People stop looking to management to make all of the key decisions and start relying on one another.

It engages people as active partners in the production of products and services. They begin to see their coworkers as allies, working together to attain mutually held objectives.

In resurrecting the Dana culture of the 1970's, Convis will likely demonstrate Aristotle's counsel to Alexander: *one* can be a very great number. As the designated new leader of Dana, his one voice will begin to be assimilated throughout a company of 35,000 employees.

Learn to play well with others. The lessons from kindergarten tend to be forgotten as adults. Yet those basic lessons are the heart of a vital and enduring organization.

July/Aug 2008

Successfully leading a vital organization has much to do with social intelligence. How you lead as a person is often more important for organizational outcomes than what you know. In this issue, we feature those valuable personal attributes that constitute high social intelligence—the intelligence we all learned in kindergarten when we learned to play well with others.

We may all readily recognize from personal experience two kinds of leaders in the work place: those we like and those we don't.

In his recent book, *Social Intelligence*, Daniel Goleman has compiled a list of attributes that characterize both of these types of leaders. The list seems to have universal appeal. He has asked people in dozens of groups around the world—from schoolteachers to CEOs—how they would describe a good boss versus a bad one.

Their answers are remarkably consistent. The good bosses are those with high social intelligence—the capacity to "play well" with others. The bad ones have issues.

Here are his lists, compiled from various cultures:

Good	Bad
Great listener	Blank wall
Encourager	Skeptic
Communicator	Secretive
Courageous	Intimidating
Sense of humor	Ill-tempered
Empathetic	Self-centered
Decisive	Indecisive
Takes responsibility	Blames others
Humble	Arrogant
Shares leadership	Mistrustful

If you want to engender enthusiasm and create a vital organization, then learn to move toward the attributes on the left. You could use the above lists for a 360-degree review. Get candid feedback from the people around you about how they perceive your style of interaction. These are polar opposites on a continuum. Ask people to rate your position on that continuum.

Learn to play well with others. The lessons from kindergarten tend to be forgotten as adults. Yet those basic lessons are the heart of a vital and enduring organization.

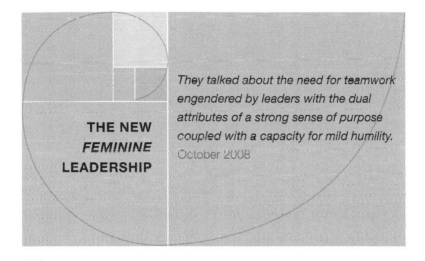

THE NEW FEMININE LEADERSHIP

They talked about the need for teamwork engendered by leaders with the dual attributes of a strong sense of purpose coupled with a capacity for mild humility.

October 2008

I recently listened to some prestigious participants in a panel discussion on "Leadership" offered by the Harvard Business School. The panel included representatives from a wide range of enterprises—from G.E. to the World Bank.

Their conversation drifted from the current political contest, to the global financial crisis, to the role of the United States as a world leader, and finally to the qualities that make for a brilliant leader.

Their conclusions were simple and profound: The world stage has just shifted—permanently; Wall Street no longer houses the "captains of the universe;" the epicenter of the global economy is moving East.

People coming to adulthood in the United States have lost the presumptive advantage. Other countries are building comparable or better schools; other countries are growing competing industries that will flourish with lower labor rates; other centers of entrepreneurial growth are eclipsing the United States as the dominant source of innovation.

What is the comparative advantage that will keep the U.S. in the game? The group seemed to concur: *leadership*. When we think of leadership, we might conjure up an image of Teddy Roosevelt passionately leading his "rough riders" in a daring charge over a hill. But that is not the kind of leadership this group had in mind.

Some talked about new qualities that contrasted sharply with the traditional masculine, command-and-control, take-charge paradigms. They talked about leaders well versed in the humanities—people with strong characters eager to build the strong characters of others. They talked about the need for *teamwork* engendered by leaders with the dual attributes of a strong sense of purpose coupled with a capacity for mild humility.

They spoke of a more *feminine* paradigm for leadership. The one-sided masculine paradigm that has dominated business cultures suppresses innovation. Leaders must create a social context where people can bring their best, where they can be free to be responsive, nimble, creative, thoughtful, and visionary. They talked about the crucial need for leaders to *invite,* not dictate, innovation and to leverage their innovation through closely-knit teams of independently minded individuals.

The leaders who engender innovative teamwork, who cultivate strong character in others, who are open to new ideas, who share leadership with many, and who have the humility to be nobody's "boss" are precisely the kind of leaders who will generate vital, innovative, and enduring organizations—*anywhere* in the world.

Leadership: Follow Through

Capitalizing on Success

Change in organizations is often most easily accomplished by affirming what is already going well, and then doing more of it. You could use the space below to note the essays on leadership that highlight your current success and also what more you might do to build on that success.

Essay Title	What else could be done?

Fixing Problems

While affirming and capitalizing on success may be the easiest way to grow collaborative genius, problems may also have to be addressed. You could use the space below to note essays that have highlighted impediments to growing collaborative genius, and what you might do to address them.

Essay Title	What could be done?

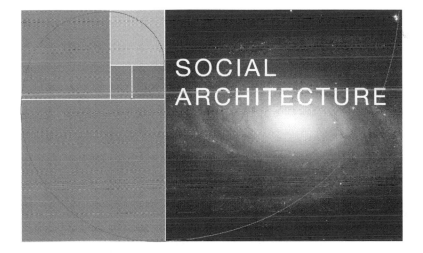

SOCIAL
ARCHITECTURE

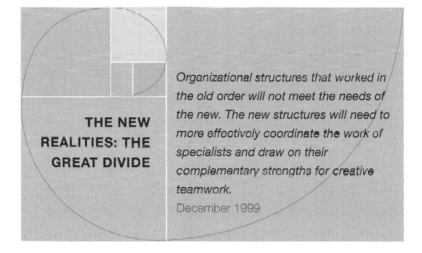

THE NEW REALITIES: THE GREAT DIVIDE

Organizational structures that worked in the old order will not meet the needs of the new. The new structures will need to more effectively coordinate the work of specialists and draw on their complementary strengths for creative teamwork.
December 1999

In his persuasive book, *The New Realities*, Peter Drucker outlines the dramatic changes occurring in virtually all walks of life. He describes a new world order already upon us, well in advance of the much-heralded new millennium. The new order will directly impact each of us individually and the organizations we join.

History illuminates epochal divides—dramatic transitional periods when the creeds and paradigms that gird the social structure are dramatically altered. For Drucker, the most recent divide occurred sometime between 1965 and 1973 when the world was ushered into a social, economic, and political *terra incognita*.

Governments across the globe lost their effectiveness to deliver the ideal society. The world grew increasingly pluralistic with multiple power centers, each concerned with its own vested social task. Existing economic theories could no longer account for the highly complex and unpredictable relationships among economic forces.

For Drucker, the most significant change was the rise of the specialist in a knowledge-based society. The more rigid command-

and-control organizations that, in their day, served highly effective and productive purposes, no longer met the needs of the new realities.

Organizational structures that worked in the old order will not meet the needs of the new. The new structures will need to more effectively coordinate the work of specialists and draw on their complementary strengths for creative teamwork.

Organizational structures in the new order will need to accommodate highly independent team members in working cooperatively toward common objectives. The most successful structures in this new environment will be those most capable of supporting cooperative teamwork among diverse people with highly specialized knowledge.

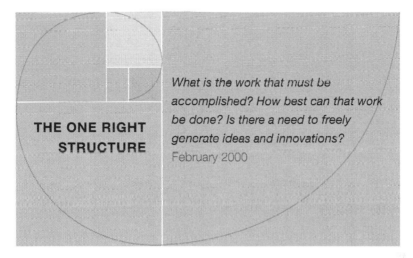

THE ONE RIGHT STRUCTURE

What is the work that must be accomplished? How best can that work be done? Is there a need to freely generate ideas and innovations?

February 2000

Wouldn't it be nice if every organization followed the same organizational structure—the *right* one?

The idea that there is one "right" management structure is one of the retarding paradigms from the last century that must be challenged, as Peter Drucker does in his insightful book, *Management Challenges for the 21st Century*. It is one of the implicit assumptions that must now be reconsidered for organizations to thrive in new operating environments.

We hear much today about the end of hierarchy in organizations. We hear that teamwork is the new and improved approach. In many situations, teamwork is the preferred mode, but not always. Hierarchy has its disadvantages, yet there are times, especially in a crisis, when hierarchy is essential.

What is the one "right" organizational structure? It does not exist. What is paramount is that the structure *fit the need*. A fundamental purpose of structure is to support people in being productive. Sometimes a hierarchical structure is better, and even absolutely necessary. Sometimes a highly flexible team approach may be ideal and necessary.

The key is to understand the nature of the work. Any structure has its strengths and deficiencies. What is the work that must be accomplished? How best can that work be done? Is there a need to freely generate ideas and innovations? If so, a more loosely structured team approach may fit the need.

Is there a need to produce a routine product or service efficiently without much interaction? Then a hierarchical approach may better suit the need. Organizations may need to engage both modes, at different times, depending on the situation. Or some hybrid combination of the two may be the best fit.

What is the one right organizational structure? It is the one that fits the need and supports the members of the organization most effectively.

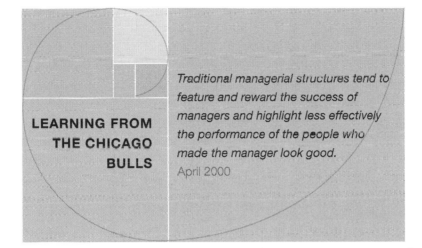

LEARNING FROM THE CHICAGO BULLS

Traditional managerial structures tend to feature and reward the success of managers and highlight less effectively the performance of the people who made the manager look good.
April 2000

So much occurs at an unconscious level to promote either harmony or conflict that it is often difficult to know when a group is really going to work well together, no matter how much training in teamwork they may have received. Yet, by studying highly successful teams, we get some important clues about the necessary elements for cooperative teamwork.

The structure for team interaction often has a remarkable effect on team results. Groups that are structured to highlight the performance of the "star" are not likely to cooperate as vitally as those focused on the performance of everyone on the team.

Traditional structures tend to feature and reward the success of managers and highlight less effectively the performance of the people who made the manager look good. The pay disparity between management and people doing frontline work can be egregiously inequitable. Disproportionately highlighting the performance of managers in a hierarchical structure tends to suppress collaboration.

Groups organized to effectively highlight and reward everyone in the group often come alive with a renewed passion for collaboration. Exemplifying such teamwork are the NBA champions, the Chicago Bulls. They could have easily organized their team around their standout star, Michael Jordan, the player widely considered to be the best ever. But they did not.

Drawing inspiration from Zen Buddhism and Lakota warriors, their unorthodox coach Phil Jackson developed a highly collaborative team structure that liberated them to respond as a cohesive group.

Using their unconventional "system," they often confounded the opposition. Their system permitted the group intelligence to emerge while it liberated the spontaneous initiatives of each individual player. To engage the system, to get lost in the "dance" of working together, each player had to embrace the idea of *selflessness* wholeheartedly.

Selflessness and traditional organizational structures are often incongruous models. One promotes the value of every one in the group; the other features the star manager. To evoke lively and flexible teamwork in organizations, we can look to the system of the Chicago Bulls that highlighted selfless teamwork rather than the star.

PRODUCTIVITY IN THE NEW ECONOMY

Traditional assumptions about compensation systems, operating structures, accounting principles, working hours, team formation, communication modes, and physical proximity will all be challenged as the new era of knowledge workers takes hold.

February 2001

Our understanding of productivity in the new economy is comparable to the understanding of industrial productivity in 1900—we barely perceive the needed changes ahead. In his recent book, *Management Challenges for the 21st Century*, Drucker has provided a glimpse of six factors that will be important for enhancing productivity of "knowledge workers" in the new economy:

1. Defined Roles

People need to know what is expected of their contribution to the whole. The intended objectives need to be well articulated.

2. Self-management

Knowledge workers increasingly need autonomy to manage their individual productivity.

3. Perpetual Innovation

Constant innovation will increasingly become a way of life—adapting to new circumstances, abandoning vestigial modes of operating, developing new approaches to enhance productivity.

4. Continuous Learning

People will need to keep learning, staying abreast of new information in their areas of competence. Some of that learning will also require teaching others, contributing to the learning of the larger group.

5. Quality *and* Quantity

The quantity of work will be no more important than the quality of the work. The quality of the work of a few people will often dramatically influence the productivity of others.

6. Assets, not Costs

Knowledge workers are among the more valuable assets of the enterprise and will increasingly be regarded as resources rather than employee expenses.

The structure of organizational relationships must respond to these emerging realities. Traditional assumptions about evaluation techniques, compensation systems, operating structures, management, accounting principles, working hours, team formation, communication modes, and physical proximity will all be challenged as the new era of knowledge workers takes hold.

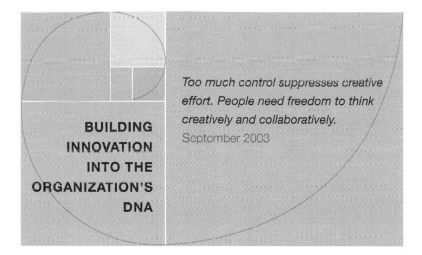

BUILDING INNOVATION INTO THE ORGANIZATION'S DNA

Too much control suppresses creative effort. People need freedom to think creatively and collaboratively.

September 2003

To continually meet the needs of an unpredictable and rapidly changing operating environment, the social architecture of an organization needs to be built with collaborative innovation in mind. Innovation is more likely to occur when catalytic systems are in place to promote creative thinking.

Some organizations discourage collaborative innovation simply in the way they organize people. Departmental silos, overbearing control, or restricted roles can be implicit in the structure itself. Collaborative thinking can also be suppressed in the way people are rewarded for their work. If compensation structures do not have incentives based on group results, people are less likely to go the extra mile of collaboration.

Every organization that truly wants to build collaborative innovation into its core culture must find systematic ways of removing the structural obstacles that keep innovation suppressed. Management control may need to be one of the first obstacles addressed in this process. Too much control suppresses creative effort. People need freedom to think creatively and collaboratively.

3M Co is a well-regarded example of how this can occur. People are invited to allocate part of their time to independent work on whatever interests them. They are encouraged to explore innovation. 3M Co. supports new ideas with a venture capital fund and expects 30% of revenues to come from new product innovations.

Do you value collaborative innovation in your organization? If so, how does the social architecture support it? Do people have time to explore innovation? Do they meet regularly, from all sectors of the company, to talk about what needs to change? Is innovation acknowledged and rewarded systematically? Is it easy for people to offer ideas *and* for those ideas to get swiftly developed and implemented? Are incentives in place to reward collaborative innovation?

Successfully addressing these questions can build collaborative innovation into the DNA of the social architecture and regenerate organizational vitality.

Innovation springs from diversity and the absence of bureaucratic controls, so we must consistently engage in what Joseph Schumpeter, the Austrian economist, called "creative destruction."
November 2003

We have all seen the familiar hierarchical chart that assigns people to their respective departmental boxes. The chart may create a sense of order and lines of responsibility, but it also tends to build confining operational silos into the structure of the organization.

Organizational charts, like fixed walls in an office layout, tend to confine dynamic interaction. The tendency to organize, to regulate, to define, to position is in us all. But it must be tempered by the need to interact without restriction, without regard to hierarchy or organizational structure.

Innovation springs from diversity and the absence of bureaucratic controls, so we must consistently engage in what Joseph Schumpeter, the Austrian economist, called "creative destruction." We must creatively destroy the barriers, the implicit rules, and standards that thwart innovation.

Rigid organizational charts are saturated with implicit rules about relationships—who may talk to whom, who may tell whom what to do. Once created, they become unconscious impediments to the free flow of information through the organization.

It is better to have a sketch, a vignette of key relationships for a variety of circumstances. It is better to create roles than reporting positions, to describe the value people bring to the party rather than who is one rung higher on the organizational ladder. Competent people do not need to be managed by a "boss." They need freedom to think, create, and interact with other competent people.

The conventional organizational chart needs to be expressed in new and more innovative ways. It needs to capture the complexity of relationships that help creative organizations thrive. It needs to clarify roles and the value delivered by those roles, but it does not need to do what it has too often done: build restraining silos into the social architecture of the organization.

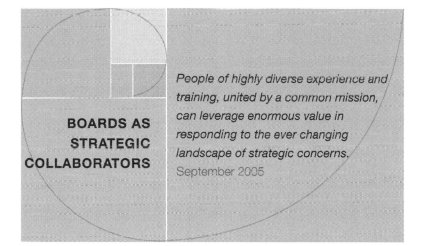

BOARDS AS STRATEGIC COLLABORATORS

People of highly diverse experience and training, united by a common mission, can leverage enormous value in responding to the ever changing landscape of strategic concerns.
September 2005

T he recently published book, *Governance as Leadership,* identified one of the key dilemmas faced by nonprofit organizations. Board members are often eager to do meaningful work but get mired in administrative detail. The board's vast potential in human and social capital—among the strongest assets of the organization—is insufficiently tapped. While their book focuses on nonprofit organizations, their message is applicable to all organizations.

At the heart of the problem is the definition of the board's role. Some see a tightly limited fiduciary role that strictly circumscribes the board's relationship to management. Others see a detailed and active role in management for the board, sometimes creating a conflagration of ill will among paid staff. Somewhere between those two extremes, boards may flounder in uncertainty about their optimal role.

Meanwhile, in the confusion, their bountiful assembled wisdom, knowledge, experience, training, and expertise are wasted and board members tire of trivial detail.

Where is the solution to this perplexing dilemma? The authors of *Governance as Leadership* recommend adopting a more vital role as *strategic collaborators*.

The role of fiduciary agent need not consume all of the board's time. With appropriate "dash board gauges" in place to monitor the organization's activity, standing committees consisting of qualified individuals can readily review the relevant fiduciary issues.

The full board's docket could be free of detailed administrative review or meddlesome operational decision-making. Bright and capable managers need the freedom to assume full responsibility for their managerial role, without the need for continually seeking permission or approval from an excessively watchful board.

A more valuable role for the board is as *strategic collaborator* with management. Sorting out the cues and clues of important strategic issues is difficult work and requires the perspectives of many. Management often feels swamped by the day-to-day operational details. It is hard to get one's head above water to consider the larger issues of strategic thinking.

The board has the needed larger perspective. People of highly diverse experience and training, united by a common mission, can leverage enormous value in responding to the ever changing landscape of strategic concerns.

ORDER VERSUS CONTROL: GEESE OR PYRAMIDS?

Is your organization light with the natural order of the geese or heavy with the control of a pyramid? Choose the way of the geese and watch the vitality of your organization soar.

August/September 2006

The traditional organizational structure is often depicted as a series of boxes indicating lines of authority and control. While these charts can be helpful in delineating reporting relationships, they can also do much to suppress organizational vitality.

The box-and-line diagram can implicitly create certain unproductive dynamics: superior/subordinate hierarchies, operational silos, "not my job" mentalities, and bureaucracy. Bureaucratic controls suppress innovation and personal initiative.

The differences between *control* and *order* must be made clear. We create trouble for ourselves by confusing the two.

Think of the V-shape that geese make as they unite to make their migratory journey. It is a natural *ordering* system that enables each of the geese to make the journey with greater ease. The geese share the more difficult point position while their aggregate wing formation reduces wind resistance for the rest of the flock.

Their V-shaped formation is a good metaphor for a well-ordered organization that is not highly controlled. It is flexible, organic, responsive, and collaborative; many take the lead role.

Organizations that function with natural ordering systems are *leader-full* organizations where anyone, from any sector of the organization, can freely take initiative. They tend to be ordered more by enthusiasm, ideas, knowledge, and talents than hierarchies of control. They are like the geese that order themselves flexibly while moving toward a common mission.

Now think of the ancient pyramids of Egypt. They could be the metaphor for an organizational hierarchy heavy with *control*. They are rigid with one fixed point of leadership at the top. The stones don't move.

The metaphor of the geese suggests order with little control, liberating personal initiative. The metaphor of the pyramid suggests order with much control, suppressing personal initiative.

Is your organization light with the natural order of the geese or heavy with the control of a pyramid? Choose the way of the geese and watch the vitality of your organization soar.

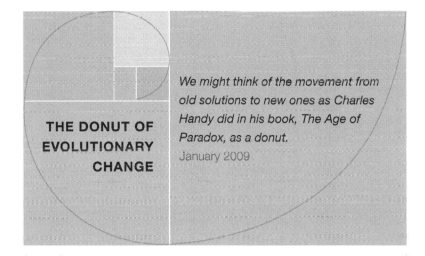

THE DONUT OF EVOLUTIONARY CHANGE

We might think of the movement from old solutions to new ones as Charles Handy did in his book, The Age of Paradox, as a donut.

January 2009

T he aim is neither big government nor small government, said Barack Obama in his inaugural address, but a government that *works*. With that simple, pragmatic statement, Obama transcended an old paradigm that induced division, creating a new one that may illicit greater unity of purpose.

Similarly, every organization must transcend the old business-as-usual paradigms that hold them in the grip of outmoded practices.

The "learn-talk-create" model for organizational progress, developed by Partners for Innovation, enables people across all segments of an organization to find the outmoded practices and presumptions holding them back, and to transcend those practices with new solutions that work.

Yet, just as President Obama will not be shutting down the wheels of government as his administration seeks the new pragmatic solutions that work, neither can an organization dismiss all of the tried and true systems that must be sustained for organizational vitality.

The movement from the old to the new is incremental. It does not take a revolution; it takes an *evolution*. We might think of the movement from old solutions to new ones as Charles Handy did in his book, *The Age of Paradox*, as a *donut*.

Consider the donut's two fundamental elements—the ring and the hole—as two modes of organizational thinking.

The hole keeps the organization "whole." It sustains the tried and true operating systems required for the organization to function. All of the practices, the methodologies, the systems, and structures that are currently operational are sustained there.

The thinking required to keep the organization "whole" is a very pragmatic approach that relies on organizational norms, standards, and traditions to sustain day-to-day operations. Everyone knows what to do and does it routinely well.

Yet, every organization must also address its need for perpetual innovation. No time in our history could bring that message home more clearly than the current economic crisis where even tried-and-true corporate giants like GM are on their stiff knees, having sustained business as usual to arthritic excess.

To stay nimble, vital, and responsive, an organization must also perpetually engage in the evolutionary change that learning, talking, and creating will engender. Every day, week, month, or year is another opportunity for strategic innovation or continual improvement.

We could think of the outer donut ring as the thinking required to push the envelope, to make incremental improvements, to learn from experience and to change. The thinking required for change in the outer ring is virtually opposite the thinking required in the hole. The "change thinking" in the ring seeks possibilities; the "no-change thinking" in the hole seeks standards and norms.

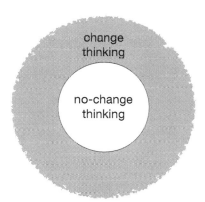

Yet both modes of thinking are required to sustain the viability of the organization. The donut grows, expands, and evolves as the possibility thinking pushes ever outward to the next incremental improvement or strategic innovation.

These modes of thinking must maintain a healthy, symbiotic balance, just as the donut hole is always symbiotically joined to the donut ring. If no-change thinking prevails, the donut becomes fossilized; if change thinking runs rampant, the donut can lose its center.

Out of that tension of opposing aspirations, highly innovative and cohesive organizations evolve at a viable midpoint between the two extremes. October 20007

We want our organizational cultures to be cohesive and united around mission and values. The composite identity of the organization depends upon people responding to stakeholders and customers consistently. We want to sustain strong cultural values that are adopted by everyone in the organization.

At the same time, we want individuals to take the initiative, to think "outside the box," to venture out in pursuit of the next best way to deliver the value of the organization. The viability of our organizations depends upon everyone's creative individual efforts.

We want our organizations to function like a herd of buffalo *and* independent stray cats—*simultaneously*.

These opposing aspirations create a healthy organizational tension. The oppositional tension *itself* keeps the culture vital. Out of that tension of opposing aspirations, highly innovative *and* cohesive organizations evolve at a viable *middle way* between the two extremes.

The two approaches are not mutually exclusive. You can have a cohesive organization with shared values and a common mission;

and people can be liberated to think creatively about their work, seize opportunities for innovation, and take the initiative to implement them.

How does that work operationally? It works differently for each organization. The balanced middle way depends on the weight of the issues involved. What is the work? Who are the people? How much quality control is necessary for a process? What are the consequences for errors? Is it routine or creative work?

These are among the issues that alter the middle way in different situations. There is no cookie cutter right answer for every organization, and every organization will likely change over time. Yet the goal is always the same: find the midpoint that successfully resolves this perpetual tension of opposing aspirations: collective norms *and* individual initiative.

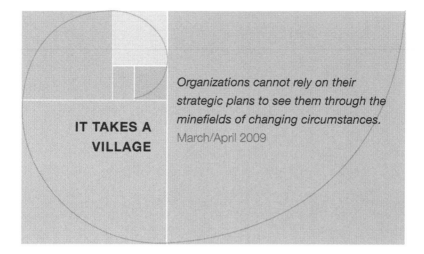

IT TAKES A VILLAGE

Organizations cannot rely on their strategic plans to see them through the minefields of changing circumstances.
March/April 2009

The Italian hill towns of Tuscany and Umbria provide an engaging metaphor for modern, adaptive organizational structures. The hill towns were built as responsive communities. They followed the contours of the terrain; they grew and evolved organically; they created multiple opportunities for informal relationships.

The industrial revolution of the 19th century modeled organizations after the dominant paradigm of their time—military hierarchies. That worked. The organizations born out of the 19th and 20th centuries, with fearsome productivity, conquered the developing world.

They knew their objectives; they understood their strategies and tactics for accomplishing them. The generals of top management grasped the long distance view and marshaled the foot soldiers of production to attain strategic objectives. Middle management carried out orders and reported results to top management. It all worked. That management model changed the modern world.

But it does not work so well now.

We need a new model for managing organizations in this new world of unexpected and tumultuous change. We are now living, in this "Great Recession," amid the paroxysm of upheaval that we might expect to be an increasingly regular part of life. We must learn to begin to expect unexpected turmoil.

The world around us will not change less frequently in the years to come; it will change *more* frequently. Organizations cannot rely on their strategic plans to see them through the minefields of changing circumstances. They must become more fluid and responsive than the old command-and-control models allow.

The managerial eyes and ears of organizations cannot be confined to "top" management. The eyes and ears attentive to changing circumstances must be everywhere, for with unexpected change comes unexpected opportunity. The vital, enlivening, sustaining work of the innovative organization is to seize opportunities amid changing circumstances, not just manage the flow of work.

A new operational paradigm can be far more effective in seizing opportunity amid rampant change: *a village*. In a village, everyone is linked; people talk and they share information. People are connected informally to others in diverse ways. They share a common cause—sustaining the life of the village. No one individual is "in charge" of the life of the village. Everyone is.

When we begin to think of our organizations as organic villages, networks, or communities, everything changes. The role of "management" shifts from controller to facilitator. The goal is not just to do the day-to-day work, but also to inform the community of budding change and emerging opportunity. Ironically, the *medieval* Italian hill town can serve as a guiding paradigm for thriving in tumultuous and unnerving modern times.

Social Architecture: Follow Through

Capitalizing on Success

Change in organizations is often most easily accomplished by affirming what is already going well, and then doing more of it. You could use the space below to note the essays on social architecture that highlight your current success and also what more you might do to build on that success.

Essay Title	What else could be done?

Fixing Problems

While affirming and capitalizing on success may be the easiest way to grow collaborative genius, problems may also have to be addressed. You could use the space below to note essays that have highlighted impediments to growing collaborative genius, and what you might do to address them.

Essay Title	What could be done?

SOCIAL
CAPITAL

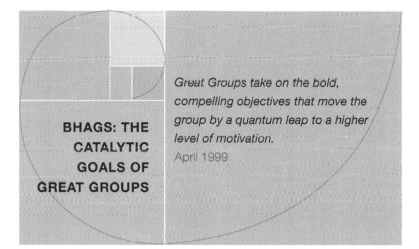

BHAGS: THE CATALYTIC GOALS OF GREAT GROUPS

Great Groups take on the bold, compelling objectives that move the group by a quantum leap to a higher level of motivation.

April 1999

Great Groups are those groups that function effectively and extraordinarily as a team. They manage to cultivate and coordinate the individual brilliance of their members for concerted, collaborative, and purposeful *action.*

These groups differ markedly from their cousins and age-old nemeses of creative efforts, the dreaded *committees*—the groups that proverbially set out to design a horse and end up with a camel. They tend to consume productive time with few productive results.

What is the difference between a Great Group and a camel-designing committee? This is one of the crucial questions that all organizations must ask if they are to cultivate their own collaborative genius.

One outstanding feature of Great Groups is what the authors of *Built to Last* refer to as BHAGs—Big Hairy Audacious Goals. Great Groups take on the bold, compelling objectives that move the group by a quantum leap to a higher level of motivation. The BHAG lives in the organization, like a hovering phantom, and engenders an unprecedented reservoir of camaraderie and energy.

In their book, *Organizing Genius*, Warren Bennis and Patricia Ward Biederman document seven Great Groups of the twentieth century. The groups were diverse, from the Disney design team that created Snow White to the Manhattan Project that produced the atom bomb. But there were a few key common denominators among these seven groups.

Among those common denominators were BHAGs. All of the seven Great Groups sought some daring, bold, audacious accomplishment that rallied enthusiasm, dedication to the work, and commitment to each other.

What is the BHAG in your organization that would catapult the group to an audacious commitment? Find it and watch the catalyst of a BHAG bring renewed commitment and passion to your culture.

WHY CAN'T THEY BE LIKE WE WERE?

What does all this mean for those who want to relate effectively to their constituency or to their team members? It means that it will often be necessary to constantly reevaluate our assumptions about world outlooks and value systems..

August 1999

We often presume that others share our values and worldview. Yet the worldview of differing generations of Americans, let alone differing cultures, can be dramatically incongruous.

Though it is hard to generalize about any group of people, generations of Americans subject to similar cultural influences will often develop similar perspectives about the world. Differences among generations are often most pronounced for deeply held beliefs and values. Consider for example, the wave of Americans graduating high school next year.

Year 2000 graduates were born in the early 1980's. They have no meaningful recollection of the Reagan Era; they can only remember one president; "Black Monday" in 1987 is as significant to them as the Great Depression; their lifetime has always included the threat of AIDS; they were about ten years old when the Soviet Union collapsed and do not remember the "Cold War;" the Vietnam War is ancient history; they have no idea that Americans were ever held hostage in Iran; they have always had access to personal computers, compact discs, cable TV, VCR's, Walkman, and answering machines; they cannot fathom not having a remote control; and MTV has been around since the beginning of their time.

What does all this mean for those who want to relate effectively to their constituency or to their team members? It means that it will often be necessary to constantly reevaluate our assumptions about world outlooks and value systems.

We can never effectively understand those value systems by viewing them from afar. We must get close, through active dialogue in one form or another. Focus groups, individual interviews, personal conversations, surveys to some degree, all help to fill out the picture of personal values and perspectives. Without that full underlying understanding of the people we are seeking to serve, sell, or work with, we will too often find ourselves stuck in the blind alley of false assumptions.

Marvin Moore

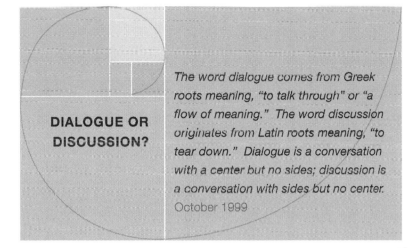

Does your group engage in dialogue or discussion? The difference can have an extraordinary impact on the results of collaboration within your organization.

The word *dialogue* comes from Greek roots meaning, "to talk through" or "a flow of meaning." The word *discussion* originates from Latin roots meaning, "to tear down." Dialogue is a conversation with a center but no sides; discussion is a conversation with sides but no center.

William Isaacs, author of *Dialogue, The Art of Thinking Together,* distinguishes dialogue from discussion using metaphorical "containers" for conversation. The first two containers characterize discussion.

Container I: Politeness

People generally follow the social rules of the organization, where it is implicitly understood that conversation will remain at a surface level, where people will not reveal what they are really thinking. Social norms control individual expression—people follow the politically correct rules of social interaction.

Container II: Breakdown

People disregard the social pressures to conform and express their positions and emotions with brutal candor. People may stubbornly engage in a verbal struggle to defend their power, position or point of view.

The other two containers, rarely attained, are forms of dialogue.

Container III: Reflective

People are willing to question their own positions—to acknowledge that they may *not* have all the right answers. They are willing to re-examine implicit assumptions that may be governing their views. Participants allow a larger meaning to begin to unfold by "talking though" values and perspectives.

Container IV: Generative

Ideas tend to flow freely without a sense of attachment or owner-ship. People become aware of acting together as an undivided whole; they listen to the views of others without judgment and freely build on one another's ideas.

Learning to transcend the first two containers and to find a way to the second two evokes the collaborative genius of people. Dia-logue has an almost magical way of delivering brilliant ideas while eliciting commitment and enthusiasm.

SUSPENDING JUDGMENT: THE THRESHOLD TO DIALOGUE

In dialogue, questions are not used to manipulate or position, they are asked as part of an authentic and honest inquiry. Authentic questions cause the group to pause and consider alternative views.

November 1999

In the October issue, we talked about dialogue versus discussion and how, in order to become fully vital and effective, groups need to transcend discussion and move to dialogue. But how do you move a whole group from one level of cooperation to another? That is the key questions that, if answered successfully, can move a group from conflict to cooperation.

There are many answers to that question. At the heart of the matter, however, is the idea that people in the group must feel they are *honored and valued.* An absence of personal judgment, as religionists throughout the centuries have told us, is fundamental to valuing and honoring others.

Dialogue only occurs when there is a willingness to listen without judgment.

Real listening occurs when one's ego position is set aside. In dialogue, questions are not used to manipulate or position, they are asked as part of an authentic and honest inquiry. Authentic questions cause the group to pause and consider alternative views.

These questions must be asked and answered without judgment. Unless people put their own preconceived opinions and perspectives aside, a more vital, more inclusive dialogue will not likely occur.

Dialogue without judgment occurs too seldom but when it does occur, it is memorable. People are often awakened to a new way of working with others—a way that can be compellingly inviting.

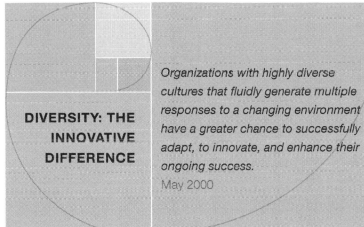

DIVERSITY: THE INNOVATIVE DIFFERENCE

Organizations with highly diverse cultures that fluidly generate multiple responses to a changing environment have a greater chance to successfully adapt, to innovate, and enhance their ongoing success.

May 2000

The life and death of industries and organizations could be compared to the struggle for new life observed in biological evolution. The survival and adaptation of organizations, like the survival and adaptation of species, depends largely on *diversity*.

The evolution of a species is dependent on multiple choices—a diverse pool of alternative adaptations—that may help a species respond more effectively to a changing environment. The more choices generated, the greater the probability of successful adaptation.

Similarly, organizations with highly diverse cultures, that are fluidly generating multiple responses to a changing environment, also have a greater chance to successfully adapt, to innovate, and enhance their ongoing success.

The whole idea of diversity within organizations often goes against the grain of conventional organizational culture. Diversity is traditionally not cultivated in organizations. In fact, it is often implicitly discouraged. If people don't "fit," they are usually expelled, one way or another, from a rigidly homogeneous organization.

Also, the traditional command-and-control approaches to management often inhibit the ongoing diversity essential for responding to a changing environment. No wonder so many large corporations today seem to be scrambling to find ways to function as smaller and more flexible entrepreneurial teams.

Generating diversity is a new concept for many, but it has been the seasoned approach to innovation for organic life. We could all do well by paying attention to that natural and persistently successful way of responding to change.

For those companies that must become highly responsive and innovative, a culture that breeds diverse views and preferably dissent at all levels of the organization will be those most likely to thrive.

October 2000

The common wisdom tells us that all organizations need well-crafted statements of vision, mission, and core values. They need to let everyone in the company know "what page we are on."

Many of the highly successful companies of the past century have been those that have promoted uniformity, loyalty and adherence to company expectations. These types of tenaciously uniform corporate cultures have been very successful at implementing innovation and carrying out large projects.

But are these cultures successful at generating innovation from all levels of the organization in response to emerging needs and changing circumstances? Recent research suggests that they are not, for they tend to inhibit a key catalyst for responsive innovation—dissent.

When a corporate culture encourages homogeneity, as many of the successful ones have, it becomes very effective at implementing innovation generated from top management. If top management is innovative, the company is innovative. Examples of such cultures include Disney, Nordstrom, Boeing, and McDonalds—all excellent companies with uniformly excellent products or services.

But innovation in these companies tends to come from the top. The organization becomes the mechanism by which innovative ideas from the top can be steadily implemented by a uniformly loyal workforce.

And for some companies, where a product or service is not in danger of becoming obsolete, a workforce with a homogeneous perspective may be ideal.

But we no longer live in an ideal age. We live in an age of intense competition and fast-changing markets where companies must learn to innovate responsively to rapidly changing conditions.

For those companies that must become highly responsive and innovative, a culture that breeds diverse views and preferably dissent at all levels of the organization will be those most likely to thrive. Dissent is a key catalyst for responsive innovation.

It is not the common wisdom that produces disruptive innovations, but rather *challenging* that common wisdom. It is not the majority view that usually gets the brilliant new insight, but rather the minority view.

The key to cultivating a highly innovative company is developing a culture where dissent is welcome, even rewarded, but at a minimum listened to and acknowledged. For out of dissent come new and more effective approaches and sometimes, brilliant innovations.

"We must have every good idea from every man and woman in the organization; we cannot afford management styles that suppress and intimidate."
November 2000

"We are trying to get the soul and energy of a start-up into the body of a $60 billion, 114-year-old company. We must have every good idea from every man and woman in the organization; we cannot afford management styles that suppress and intimidate."

These are the words of Jack Welch—the CEO who dramatically altered the way GE does business over his nearly twenty-year term. GE accomplished much of that change with simple organizational innovations like "Work Out," "Best Practices," and "Six Sigma," innovations that transformed their culture.

Work Out is the name given to a three-day retreat of groups of fifty people from all levels of the organization that gather just to talk openly about what needs fixing in the company and in their operating environments.

Best Practices is another opportunity for people to meet and informally review what is working well. People from outside of GE are often brought in to talk about what is working in industries unrelated to GE's. It is an opportunity for cross-fertilizing and synthesizing fresh ideas into the fabric of GE's operating practices.

Six Sigma focuses on reducing defects in products and processes, setting highly ambitious goals for statistical results. The ambitious goals themselves require people to start thinking and talking about the unconventional and about new approaches to accomplishing what had been previously unattainable.

How do you get the soul and energy of a start-up in a $60 billion dollar enterprise? The same way you get that soul and energy into the body of any organization. You give people the opportunity to talk and take responsibility for what needs fixing, what is going well, and what new approaches need to be developed.

Simple. Like all highly effective innovation, the answer is usually simple.

You can't believe how hard it is for people to be simple, how much they fear being simple. They worry that if they're simple, people will think they're simple-minded. In reality, of course, it's just the reverse. Clear, tough-minded people are the most simple.

Jack Welch

Virtually all of the possibility is with the group where the central self prevails, where there is a critical mass of people committed to living generous, open and creative lives.
December 2000

Do you remember those times when you have been so self-absorbed that you seemed to be on a downward spiral—one that seemed to consume all the possibility in your life? Benjamin and Rosamund Zander, authors of the new book *The Art of Possibility*, describe this experience as that of our "calculating selves."

It is probably safe to say that we have all had the experience of feeling greedy, self-protective, or defensive—of taking ourselves too seriously, often to the exclusion of the needs of others. This is the experience of the calculating self. It can be disingenuous, manipulative, fearful and self-aggrandizing. But the authors also write about another experience, an experience of the "central self."

We can probably all remember experiences with this side of our lives as well. They have a far more generous and genuine feel about them. We take ourselves less seriously; we are lighter, more open, and more willing to make a contribution to others. We view the world as full of abundance rather than scarcity; we are more interested in how we can contribute than in what our share will be.

The distinction between these two is vital for collaborative innovation, for a group temperament centered in the calculating self will be unproductive, ornery, suspicious, and political. There will be precious little room for possibility or for creating anything of value.

Virtually all of the possibility is with the group where the central self prevails, where there is a critical mass of people committed to living generous, open, and creative lives.

In Charles Dickens' *A Christmas Carol*, Ebenezer Scrooge artfully illustrates these two opposing ways of life: the stingy, hoarding way of life before his transformation and the generous, creative way of life after it.

His transformation occurred when he made the conscious choice to live a generous life. With groups of people at work, it is also a choice. Sometimes the choice of just one person in the group can make the difference for everyone.

Which way do we choose? The answer seems obvious, but how much of our daily work lives is lived out of a sense of abundance and a genuine interest in the welfare of others?

The choice is ours, from minute to minute. The choice to live from that central self is full of possibility for us individually, and for the whole group.

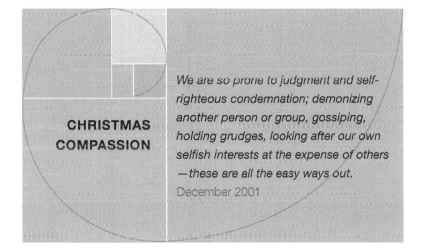

CHRISTMAS
COMPASSION

We are so prone to judgment and self-righteous condemnation; demonizing another person or group, gossiping, holding grudges, looking after our own selfish interests at the expense of others —these are all the easy ways out.

December 2001

This is the sentimental and memorable season of Christmas, when one of the major religions of the world, Christianity, celebrates the birth of Jesus of Nazareth. In the United States, the Christmas sentiment is pervasive. For many, it is a time of good cheer, happy memories, and warm family ties. The streets, shops, homes, and even the air seem enchanted with the spirit of Christmas.

This year—the year of the heart-wrenching 9/11 tragedy—it may be especially helpful to remember the essential qualities of the birth that is being celebrated. These are the essential qualities that engender understanding, dialogue, forgiveness, and compassion among diverse people.

The birth of Jesus of Nazareth and his religious life constitute one of the most exalted expressions of compassion ever born into our world. It is so exalted, in fact, that most of us find it difficult to even come close to that high ideal in our daily lives.

He taught and lived a life of forgiveness, tolerance, and positive compassion. Few have ever really practiced religion as he lived it. Fewer still are the groups that have fully embraced his compassionate religion of faith as a way of life.

Yet his approach to life is at the heart of how groups can live and work cooperatively together, in any setting. We are so prone to judgment and self-righteous condemnation; demonizing another person or group, gossiping, holding grudges, looking after our own selfish interests at the expense of others; these are all the easy ways out. They require little effort.

Just as it took less effort to destroy the World Trade Center than to build it, so it is easier to judge and condemn than to build relationships and community.

But the compassionate effort required to build relationships, to seek first to understand, to take the log out of our own eyes rather than to remove the splinter from the eyes of others, to carry someone's figurative pack for a second mile, to turn a cheek that has been struck and respond positively—this is the effort that is at the heart of the religion of Jesus of Nazareth. This is the life of compassion that was born 2000 years ago.

This is also the effort that is at the heart of developing responsive and collaborative groups of people with diverse views, talents, and personal aspirations. This effort is more difficult than selfish aggrandizement, but also more exalted. Like the Christmas season, it too fills the air.

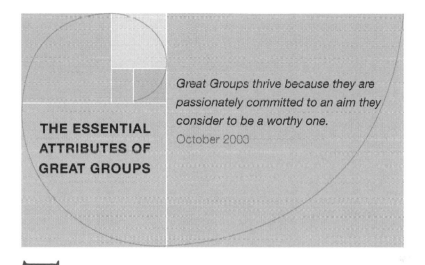

Great Groups thrive because they are passionately committed to an aim they consider to be a worthy one.

October 2000

Through his research into "Great Groups," Warren Bennis, chairman of the Leadership Institute of the University of California, has identified important attributes that characterize groups that thrive on collaborative innovation.

Bennis studied highly creative and productive groups like the artists who so beautifully illustrated the astounding full-length animated film, *Snow White*. Among these highly collegial and spectacularly productive groups, Bennis uncovered a few attributes that can serve as valuable guides for any organization seeking to develop its own "collaborative genius." Three in particular are worth emulating:

A Shared Dream

Great Groups seem to believe they are on a virtual mission from God. They have a very clear sense of purpose and heightened aspirations. Their dream of what they could create together is like a fervent quest for the Holy Grail.

Collegiality

Great Groups have a high *esprit de corps*, a revitalizing sense of collegiality. They put their common good first. They surrender self-centered pursuits to the pursuit of attaining some audacious collective goal.

Benefit to Others

Great Groups deliver some product or service that is self-evidently valuable to others. They apply their stamina, their intelligence, and their creative energy to work not for their own benefit, but for the benefit of others.

Great Groups are dedicated to purposes greater than simply sustaining their own well-being. They are committed to a grand dream of some valuable contribution to the world, and out of that commitment, their lives acquire a greater sense of significance.

The renowned psychiatrist Bruno Bettelheim once said, "Communal life can only flourish if it exists for an aim outside itself. Community is viable if it is the outgrowth of a deep involvement in a purpose which is other than, or above, that of being a community." Great Groups thrive when they are passionately committed to an aim they consider to be a worthy one.

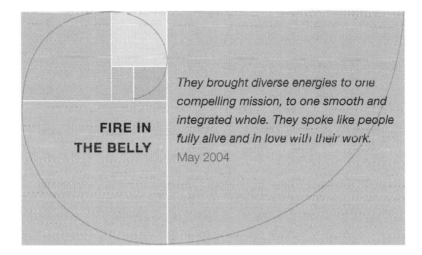

They brought diverse energies to one compelling mission, to one smooth and integrated whole. They spoke like people fully alive and in love with their work.
May 2004

We were dazzled. For some, this was their first orchestral concert. Others had never stepped foot in the grand and enchanting Peristyle concert hall. Few of us had ever witnessed a group so passionately engaged in their work. Even those who had not seen the Orpheus Chamber Orchestra "up close and personal," as we had with them on stage during their rehearsal, said they had never seen such "fire in the belly" in any orchestra.

The musicians were alive with the music; they owned it. They were main-lining the pure joy of doing what they loved to do; they knew they could each be trusted and respected to give their best to the work. They had found their collaborative genius. No wonder others have said of them that they are "...one of the great marvels of the music world."

The recent Orpheus Seminar ignited thoughts of new possibilities for all of us. How, we wondered, could we take the admirable attributes of Orpheus and transfer them to our own work?

Executive Director, a.k.a. violinist, Ronnie Bauch, imparted some intriguing clues. "We don't leave our egos at the door," he said, "We leave our insecurities. Everyone has an equal voice, but you have to earn the respect of others in the group—you earn the strength of your voice."

We, in the seminar, picked up our own clues. We noticed that they were having fun, all night long. They kidded during rehearsals, making jokes, and poking fun. They expressed frustrations freely.

During rehearsal, one or two designated leaders went out into the hall to listen to the group and make adjustments. They coached one another during rehearsal. They affirmed one another in small ways. During the performance, their eyes searched, always touching base with the other musicians, cueing one another and staying in touch.

They brought diverse energies to one compelling mission, to one smooth and integrated whole. They spoke like people fully alive and in love with their work.

"How," many of us thought, as we made our way home from our inspiring seminar with Orpheus, "could we bring this sort of trust, enthusiasm, and passion to bear in our organizations?"

Though there was not time to talk that evening, many of us will be gathering again soon, at a follow-up workshop, to talk about that very question. The next Innovation Tip will share the lessons from that workshop. We will be seeking, and no doubt finding, access to what we all silently hope for in life and in work—*fire in the belly.*

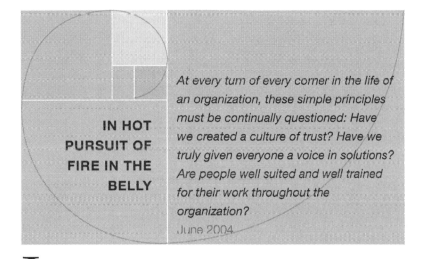

IN HOT PURSUIT OF FIRE IN THE BELLY

At every turn of every corner in the life of an organization, these simple principles must be continually questioned: Have we created a culture of trust? Have we truly given everyone a voice in solutions? Are people well suited and well trained for their work throughout the organization?

June 2004

June 28, 2004. A small group of Orpheus Chamber Orchestra enthusiasts met today to talk about how to light the Orpheus "fire in the belly" in any organizational culture. We identified many of the Orpheus attributes worth emulating:

The musicians *listen* without defending positions.

+ They are *committed* to their work and consider it important and valuable.

+ They are committed to their roles in a process rather than to titles.

+ They have a sense of pride and ownership in what they accomplish.

+ They have strong egos, but *they are not ego-centric.*

+ They fully *respect* one another.

* Each musician is supremely *competent and confident.*

* *No* suggestions are minimized or dismissed.

* There is extraordinary *trust* and *support.*

* They are *fully prepared* for their performance.

* They thrive on learning from mistakes and don't cast blame when mistakes occur.

* The people performing the music have a say in solutions.

* Work is viewed as both meaningful and valuable.

* They give each other constant feedback.

* People feel they can be creative without risk of criticism.

* Their commitment to the process transcends individualism.

* They affirm one another constantly.

From this master list, we identified a few general principles that could apply to any organization:

Trust

Create an environment where people affirm, trust, and respect one another, where they listen without defending a position, and leave their insecurities at the door.

Ownership

Make the process of dialogue more important than organizational structure or hierarchy. Give people a significant voice in generating solutions, especially the people doing the work, and give them a mission that matters.

Competence

Make sure that people are highly competent, gifted, and prepared to serve in their designated roles.

To attain the kind of passion we witnessed among the Orpheus musicians, these few attributes seemed necessary. If they are not present, we concluded, the "collaborative genius" of any group is unlikely to be realized.

At every turn of every corner in the life of an organization, these simple principles must be continually questioned: Have we created a culture of trust? Have we truly given everyone a voice in solutions? Are people well suited and well trained for their work throughout the organization?

Silently but surely, when these questions are persistently addressed, we begin to feel what so many of us hope for in life and work—*fire in the belly*. When the passion we witnessed in the Orpheus Chamber Orchestra heats up, no one wants to put the fire out.

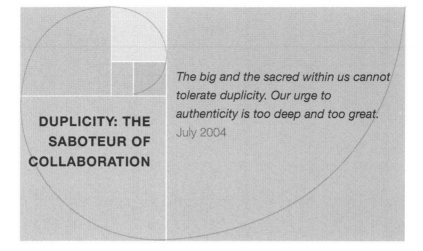

DUPLICITY: THE SABOTEUR OF COLLABORATION

The big and the sacred within us cannot tolerate duplicity. Our urge to authenticity is too deep and too great.
July 2004

People know duplicity when they see it. It does not take long for people to realize that a person's walk is different from his talk. Duplicity will dull people's enthusiasm and sabotage collaboration. No one, in his heart of hearts, wants to be part of a sham.

Most organizations have *stated* core values. Too often, those values, drafted in an isolated boardroom, do not make it from the paper they were written on to the life of the organization. Instead those words become a constant reminder that the organization is duplicitous—it claims one thing and does another.

The really successful organizations do not need written values. Their values are animated inseparably in the daily work of the organization. They are transmitted, not by words, but by *action*.

Do stated values say that people ought to respect one another? If so, you will see it, feel it, and hear it at every meeting, casually in the hallways, and in the way people talk to one another.

Do the leaders say they want a highly collaborative and innovative organization? Then they must demonstrate that commitment by giving work groups autonomy to take the initiative. They must affirm rather than control. When they do, they will see the results in people's eyes; they will feel the warmth of fire in the belly.

In highly collaborative and innovative organizations, people experience the thrill of becoming more than they ever thought they could be. Most of us long to be part of something "big and sacred." Becoming more, as teams or as individuals, than we ever thought possible is thrilling. We long for the growth to which our own potential calls us.

If we live out our lives in a duplicitous organization that *claims* to honor that compelling urge, but does not really, something within us rebels. The big and the sacred within us cannot tolerate duplicity. Our urge to authenticity is too deep and too great. Organizations that fail to truly live their intended values will breed discontent, and that discontent will sabotage collaboration.

SOCIAL CAPITAL: THE RISING TIDE FOR ALL BOATS

From industry, to science, to engineering, to physics, to art, to political initiatives, strong social capital has been the intangible ingredient for breath-taking success.

October 2004

We may be familiar with the concept of *human capital*—the value of people as assets in an organization. People individually bring the value of their training, experience, skills, and expertise; the sum total of all of that would be the human capital of the organization.

But what is the value of the *social capital* of the organization—the cooperative bonds between those people? Researchers are discovering that trust, productive conversations, a willingness to help others out, and the ability to share and develop ideas creates immeasurable value. Strong social capital not only enhances the organization's image and external relationships, it also increases the value of human capital exponentially.

Strong social capital has created personal fortunes and altered the very course of history. From industry, to science, to engineering, to physics, to art, to political initiatives, strong social capital has been the intangible ingredient for breath-taking success.

Andrew Carnegie, the early twentieth century steel magnate who started as a penniless immigrant, knew virtually nothing about the making or marketing of steel. But he gathered the right people around him who did. Simply by maintaining a cooperative working harmony among these people, he acquired more wealth in one lifetime than anyone before him. Selling his steel empire, he then spent his fortune on an elaborate infrastructure of philanthropic projects from which we still benefit today.

The remarkable accomplishments of the founding fathers of the United States were achieved largely through the strength of their social capital. Many were brilliant individuals, but together they became intellectual demigods. Certainly they had disagreements; but they had one uniting common mission that kept them cohesively on course in the creation of a new democratic nation.

The Impressionist painters of nineteenth century Europe collaborated harmoniously to change the course of European painting. They created some of the most delightful and engaging images ever painted. Monet and Renoir, two of the leading Impressionists, worked so closely together that at times their work was indistinguishable.

The engineers at Lockheed who designed and built some of the most astonishing aircraft ever made—and *invisible* to radar—did so by creating an informal collegial working environment where engineers and technicians worked side by side to develop ideas, resolve problems, and refine designs.

All of these groups attained phenomenal success by capitalizing on the free asset too often ignored in organizations—*social capital*. Engaging the magic and power of social capital—the ability of groups to work cooperatively and harmoniously together—elevates every endeavor.

Like the rising tide that raises all boats, social capital effortlessly and efficiently elevates the value of everyone's ideas, contribution, and productivity. People who learn to elevate their work through the uplift of social capital discover that they are capable of accomplishing more than they ever thought possible.

The triple spiral of social capital consists of these three indispensable elements: relationships, vision, and information. Each of these must be healthy for the organization to regenerate successfully.
November/December 2004

The DNA molecule—a double spiral (helix) as Watson and Crick discovered—is the molecule that builds all living organisms. Life in our world would not be regenerated without it. When that intricate and complex molecule goes awry, the whole organism can become terminally ill.

Similarly, in our living organizations, there is a triple spiral of conditions that build social capital. If any of the three strands of that spiral go awry, the whole organization will suffer.

The triple spiral of social capital consists of these three indispensable elements: *relationships, vision,* and *information.* Each of these must be healthy for the organization to regenerate successfully.

Relationships

The conditions for productive dialogue must be present in the way people relate to one another. Healthy organizations build a high level of trust, starting with the leadership. If the leadership cannot be trusted to be authentic and fair, to be above board and honest, the whole organization will suffer. An absence of trust in the leadership will cast a repressive pall over the whole organization.

Vision

At the heart of thriving organizations—where people are really pulling together—is a strong sense of a meaningful common purpose. Just building shareholder wealth does not cut it. Just collecting a paycheck is not enough. People need to know that their lives count for something. Enthusiasm and passion for collaborative efforts naturally unfold when people are fully aware of the value being delivered by their joint work.

Information

If there is one gnawing, persistent need that we hear in every organization we assess, it is this: the need for better communication. People want to know, *have to know*, what is going on if they are to make a meaningful and informed contribution to the life of the organization. Open and clear communication is essential. When the channels of communication dry up, so does organizational vitality.

These three strands of the social capital spiral are indispensable ingredients for organizational vitality. When they are present, all work is easier. When any one is missing, the living systems of collaborative genius get jammed.

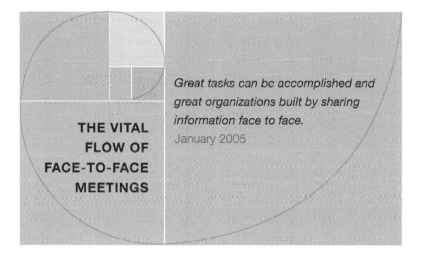

THE VITAL
FLOW OF
FACE-TO-FACE
MEETINGS

*Great tasks can be accomplished and
great organizations built by sharing
information face to face.*

January 2005

Information needs to be shared; people want and *need* to know what is going on to make meaningful and informed contributions. Research has shown that open and clear communication is critical to worker satisfaction; people who feel fully informed are much more motivated and satisfied.

To keep information open and clear, face-to-face meetings are often essential. People have been remarkably productive and innovative when information flows freely this way.

Established in 1970, the Palo Alto Research Center developed the first user-friendly computer, the first easy-to-learn word processing program, the first local computer network, and the first laser printer. They held weekly meetings to ensure that the right information made it to the right people. In this highly inventive group, there was only one rule that could not be broken: *they had to go to the weekly meetings.* These were purposeful meetings that allowed everyone to stay informed about the ideas and work of others and eliminated the need for endless reports.

A firm that started as a simple postage meter company more than 80 years ago grew to be an industry leader through the regular use of face-to-face meetings. Pitney Bowes held meetings where people freely challenged the management team. Their forums were designed to get to the truth about important company-wide issues. People clearly understood that the focus of these forums was the continual improvement of the company and they participated candidly without any fear of reprisal.

A brilliant group of scientists and engineers recruited to the Manhattan Project during World War II were initially segregated from each other and kept uninformed about the purpose of their work. They were assigned number-crunching chores and other tedious tasks—which they performed neither quickly nor well. Once informed that they had been recruited for a project that could quickly end World War II, the pace and proficiency of their work accelerated exponentially. They openly shared information in weekly meetings, for only by freely sharing information could they accomplish their Herculean task.

Great tasks can be accomplished and great organizations built by sharing information face to face. Unlike emails or reports, meetings enable people to share information in a lively and dynamic way.

Face-to-face meetings have the power to propel innovative organizations to phenomenal success if purposes are clearly stated and ideas and information are honestly shared. These are the productive and vital forums where information flows freely and where people make meaningful and informed contributions to their collective work.

Margie Spino

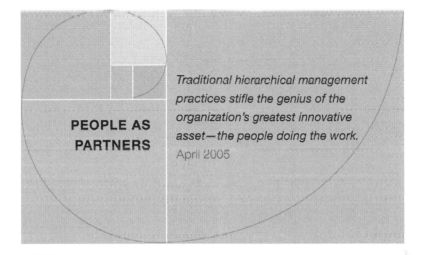

Traditional hierarchical management practices stifle the genius of the organization's greatest innovative asset—the people doing the work.
April 2005

Oe of the misfortunes of standard accounting practices is the reference to "employee expense." People, in this fiscal framework, are considered another cost of doing business. Their highest value as productive partners is suppressed when they are reduced to an implied cost rather than asset.

Those organizations that treat people as common expenses, run sweatshops, count beans rather than ideas, or manage by intimidation rather than affirmation, have short shelf lives. They may see near-term financial results rise, but they stunt the creative thought and continual improvement that will produce *long-term* results.

Traditional hierarchical management practices stifle the genius of the organization's greatest innovative asset—*the people doing the work*. The very operational terms of traditional management imply a suppressive regime—"subordinates," "supervisors," "direct reports," "boss" to name a few. The terms tend to fortify implicit hierarchies, command-and-control cultures, and political silos that impede creative collaboration.

Much more innovative and effective are the organizations that promote people as *partners*. These are the organizations, like Toyota or Southwest Airlines that sometimes stand head and shoulders above their competition. They build tremendous customer and employee loyalty while they cultivate cultures of mutual support and continual improvement.

Management at Southwest Airlines likes to say that they are building a culture of love rather than fear. Their "culture of love" has the best passenger satisfaction ratings, the best departure and arrival ratings, the best baggage handling ratings, and the best financial results in the airline industry.

Toyota is considered by many to be the best manufacturer in the world. By attending to the *Toyota Way*—a way that respects and honors employees—Toyota has grown from a fledgling family business to a immense international company. Often heard in the halls and manufacturing floors is the simple Toyota theme: "Before we build cars, we build people."

Like other companies that have attained strikingly prodigious achievement, Toyota and Southwest corroborate the value of developing *people as partners*.

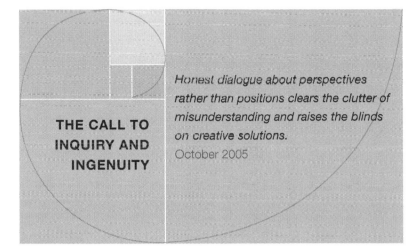

THE CALL TO INQUIRY AND INGENUITY

Honest dialogue about perspectives rather than positions clears the clutter of misunderstanding and raises the blinds on creative solutions.

October 2005

We live in a politically unsettling culture—red versus blue, Islamic versus Christian, Jew versus Arab, fundamentalism versus scientism, black versus white, democracies versus theocracies, county versus city, you versus me. Everywhere we look we seem to find conflict—*destructive conflict*.

Yet we know that conflict can be healthy. A tension of opposites is essential for personal growth. Character does not grow without adversity. Innovations are born of dissonance. The whole spiraling evolution of life—intelligently designed *or* randomly selected—depends upon *responding* successfully to conflictive events.

How then can we intentionally respond to conflict in a constructive and healthy way? The essential difference between destructive conflict and resistance that generates constructive results can be summarized in two words: *inquiry* and *ingenuity*.

Healthy conflict requires inquiry—people seeking a full understanding of the sources of conflict *together*. Honest dialogue about perspectives rather than positions clears the clutter of misunderstanding and raises the blinds on creative solutions.

The opposite of inquiry—pigheadedness—leads ultimately to an avalanche of perpetual conflict. Trust and mutual understanding slip rapidly downhill, damaging relationships along the way.

Inquiry seeks first simply to understand: What are the values behind the position? What can we do together to achieve the desired value?

Understanding between sincere people, born of honest inquiry, leads inevitably to *ingenuity*—creating viable solutions. Whether a marriage, a friendship, a workplace dilemma, or political, racial, or religious differences, the formula is always the same: *honest inquiry produces inventive ingenuity.*

When inquiry prevails, every problem becomes an opportunity; every conflict provides the potential to create something ingeniously valuable.

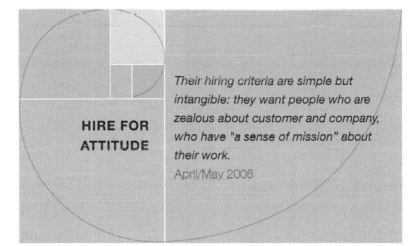

HIRE FOR ATTITUDE

Their hiring criteria are simple but intangible: they want people who are zealous about customer and company, who have "a sense of mission" about their work.

April/May 2006

H̲ave you ever watched "The Apprentice" on television? Donald Trump is often prominently featured telling someone "You're fired!" In reality, these people were never really hired.

Trump could take some tips from Southwest Airlines. Southwest Airlines has been one of the most successful organizations in America, largely because of the way people are treated, *and hired.*

Southwest doesn't hire for skills or experience; rather, they hire for *attitude* and train for skill. Southwest has a notoriously offbeat culture full of energy, humor, team spirit, and self-confidence. They search daily for people who could fit in with that culture. When they find them, they train them well and develop their skills.

Their hiring criteria are simple but intangible: they want people who are zealous about customers and their company—who have "a sense of mission" about their work.

To find the right people, they look for special qualities in unconventional ways. Their interviews can be as offbeat as their culture. They ask people to create a personal "coat of arms"—a statement that gets to the heart of a person's passion. They ask about humor, special personal achievements, and guiding principles.

Their quest is not so much to find out what the person can *do* as to know the *person*. Like the old saw, they don't care how much a person knows; they just want to know that the person cares.

This longstanding practice of their "People Department" in hiring for attitude and training for skill has served them well. The company consistently gets the highest industry ratings for virtually all of the critical performance measures. While Donald Trump might still be firing, Southwest Airlines is still hiring.

Chris Stearns

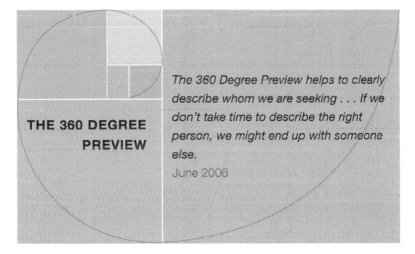

THE 360 DEGREE PREVIEW

The 360 Degree Preview helps to clearly describe whom we are seeking . . . If we don't take time to describe the right person, we might end up with someone else.

June 2006

Before bringing new people into the organization, it is important to know that they have the right aptitudes as well as the right attitudes. But how can you be sure that you have found a person with the right aptitudes?

Resumes may be impressive, but in the end it is not what people have done for others that matters most; what matters is what they can do for you. It is too easy, and too often ineffective, to hire people because they have experience with similar work.

Aptitude tests may help, yet standardized tests are never 100% reliable. Psychological preference instruments have many shortfalls and can be easily manipulated by the test taker.

Research indicates that personal interviews are among the poorest means of evaluating a candidate's potential. Too many subjective factors influence the results.

Yet each of these approaches has some value. A person's past successful experience with work confirms that the individual can do the work—whether or not the work engages their best gifts. Testing can confirm evidence of perceived aptitudes. Interviews with several people individually help to reduce the subjective influence of any one interviewer.

Each of these approaches is more effective when you have a clear understanding of the attributes being sought. Describing the attributes of the ideal person is as simple as doing a 360-degree review. Simply ask the people who will be working with this individual what attributes they would value most.

Should the person have a deeply penetrating intellect, an openness to new ideas, a high social intelligence, a facility with data and facts, an ability to adapt quickly to changing circumstances, the ability to be decisive, an aptitude to discern new and imaginative possibilities, a deep connection to enduring values?

We call this descriptive summary of the ideal attributes the "360 Degree Preview." It is a snapshot of the personal attributes considered most important. When you have a clear picture of the attributes you want, you are in a much better position to ask pertinent probing questions.

In a busy work place, we all may too often settle for just filling a position. Yet, getting the right people is an essential component of building a vital organization. It behooves us to spend the necessary time to find the right people.

The 360 Degree Preview helps to clearly describe whom we are seeking. It is a necessary step in recruiting the right people to the organization. If we don't take time to describe the right person, we might end up with someone else.

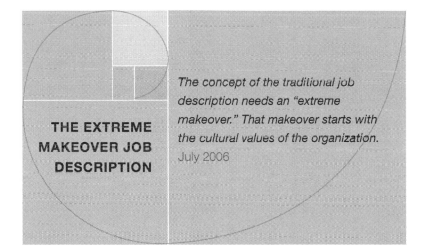

THE EXTREME
MAKEOVER JOB
DESCRIPTION

*The concept of the traditional job
description needs an "extreme
makeover." That makeover starts with
the cultural values of the organization.*
July 2006

T he tried and true "job description" must be handled with care, for job descriptions, if handled poorly, can make the right person very wrong for the right organization. The goal of the job description ought to be to liberate people rather than control them. The concept of the traditional job description needs an "extreme makeover." That makeover starts with the cultural values of the organization.

The job description ought to include the "collegial call"—a commitment to the values that create social capital in the organization. Teamwork—helping others out—is often among the most important. The extreme makeover job description does not start with tasks, it starts with *values*, for the greatest asset held by most organizations is not the sum total of their people—human capital—but the exponential value of those people working cooperatively together—their *social capital*.

The *mission* of the work also needs to be made clear. It is not as important to delineate specific job tasks, as it is to delineate the purposeful *value* of the work. Under the extreme makeover version, a receptionist's mission could be, for example, "to create great first impressions."

Finally, the description of the work in the extreme makeover job description ought to be keyed to individual gifts. We all enjoy work more fully when we are doing work that we love. If we want to generate enthusiasm everywhere in the organization, we must take some time to sculpt people's work to their best gifts.

An online job assessment is now available that enables you to assess the gifts needed for a given job. It also enables people to assess their individual gifts to see how well they match the gifts for the job (see GiftsCompass™ Inventory, www.giftscompass.com).

The purpose of that comparison is to optimize the value of the individual to the organization. The traditional job description is a holdover from the industrial age of scientific management when it was believed that efficiency equaled effectiveness.

In today's more innovative age of "knowledge workers," effectiveness is more a function of individual *gifts*. Small teams of people with complementary gifts who are *sharing* work will often outperform groups of people doing the same work individually.

The value of people to the organization is optimized when they understand that the "collegial call" to teamwork is part of their role, when they are clear about how their role contributes value to the mission of the organization, and when they are using their best gifts in concert with others to accomplish that mission.

Margie Spino / Linda DeArment

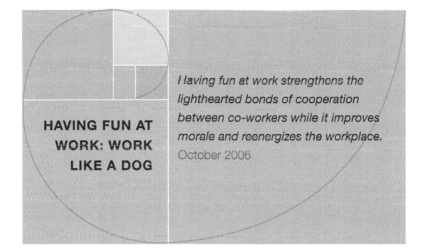

HAVING FUN AT WORK: WORK LIKE A DOG

Having fun at work strengthens the lighthearted bonds of cooperation between co-workers while it improves morale and reenergizes the workplace.
October 2006

It could probably be said of many of us that we spend more time with our co-workers than they do with our families. Wouldn't it be great if we could be as relaxed in our work environments as we are at home? We can. The solution is simple: *work like a dog.*

Dogs don't make a distinction between work and play. Everything is fun for them. They thrive on enjoying themselves. They wag their tales in a virtual nanosecond when they find a new play-mate.

We could all feel more successful and more relaxed if we would approach our work with the same enthusiasm, enjoyment, and optimism as a dog having fun. Not only do we individually feel better about our work when we are having fun, the organizations we serve do better also.

All of our consulting experience with organizations suggests that productive creativity and cutting edge innovation travel with fun like…well, like a pack of dogs. Having fun at work strengthens the lighthearted bonds of cooperation among co-workers while it improves morale and reenergizes the workplace.

Playfair, "the world's leading experts on fun and play at work" have made working like a dog a lot easier. Their annual conferences have highlighted what various companies have done to have more fun at work.

For example, the Global Service Center of MasterCard International celebrated "Dress Your Manager Day," outfitting supervisors as nuns, biker chicks, Elvis, a used car salesman, and the Joker.

EDS in Buffalo, New York recognized people with a "Manager of Mirth Award." Those who readily created fun or set a lighthearted example were acknowledged with the coveted award.

Creating a more relaxed and enjoyable work environment is sometimes simply a matter of having more fun. Don't let the stress of work be the tail that wags the dog of your well-being. Work like a dog: enjoy yourself; be eager to greet people; anticipate the day with cheerful optimism. Before you know it, the whole organization will be wagging its tail.

Chris Stearns

The supreme accomplishment is to blur the line between work and play.
Arnold Toynbee

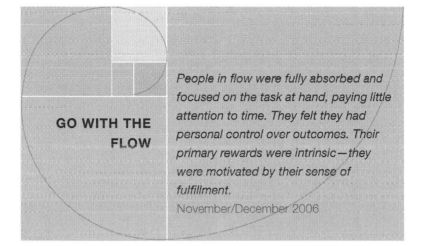

GO WITH THE FLOW

People in flow were fully absorbed and focused on the task at hand, paying little attention to time. They felt they had personal control over outcomes. Their primary rewards were intrinsic—they were motivated by their sense of fulfillment.

November/December 2006

You have heard this before: When life becomes overwhelming and challenges seem insurmountable, just go with the flow. But what is flow, and why would we want to go with it?

Dr. Mihaly Csikszentmihalyi (Mike), Director of the Quality of Life Research Center at Claremont Graduate University, describes flow as "the experience of optimal fulfillment and engagement." In studying people from all walks of life, from artists and athletes to rock climbers and writers, he consistently discovered "the deep and uniquely human motivation to excel, exceed, and triumph over limitation."

People in flow were fully absorbed and focused on the task at hand, paying little attention to time. They felt they had personal control over outcomes. Their primary rewards were intrinsic—they were motivated by their sense of fulfillment. Their experience was so richly rewarding that they wanted it again, even though it would take much time and effort.

His research showed that people were happier doing things than not, especially when their abilities were equal to the challenge.

If their ability exceeded the challenge, then they tended to get bored. If the challenge exceeded their ability, then they tended to get frustrated. For their flow to feel most fulfilling, the work needed to engage, but not exceed, their ability.

Csikszentmihalyi also noted that happiness can also be contingent upon making a contribution to the common good—to living for something more than one's own personal interest. The more meaningful the work, the greater happiness it tends to engender. With optimal personal flow, we also shape a culture that is better for all.

A key question for every organization is this: "How can we help to create the conditions of flow for ourselves and others?" We have found these guiding principles to be helpful:

* Be sure that the mission and import of the work are well understood.

* Match the work to the people with the right gifts to accomplish it. (Sometimes job sharing or job sculpting are needed to improve flow.)

* Enable people to focus on their work without distractions.

* Encourage and commend rather than micromanage.

Imagine the world we could create if we could all more often, *go with the flow.*

Margie Spino

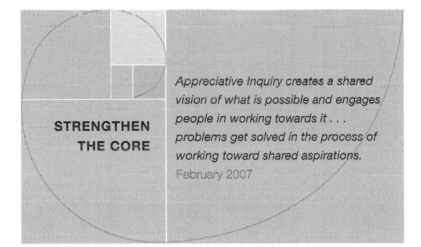

STRENGTHEN
THE CORE

Appreciative Inquiry creates a shared vision of what is possible and engages people in working towards it . . . problems get solved in the process of working toward shared aspirations.
February 2007

Fitness experts preach the importance of strengthening our physical core—those core muscles that are our body's power zone. Every movement we make originates here; keeping it strong enhances our physical abilities and protects us from injury. We need this core of strength to perform at our best. Similarly, we do well to strengthen our personal core—our zone of personal assets, competencies, stories, dreams, and achievements.

Case Western Professor of Organizational Behavior, David Cooperrider, says that there is extraordinary power to be found in strengthening the core in organizations too. When we build a strong, life-affirming core in an organization, the organization is poised to deliver its highest capabilities.

Cooperrider coined the term Appreciative Inquiry (AI) to characterize the process of developing positive cores in organizations. The premise of AI is that there is more to be gained from building strengths and common aspirations than correcting weakness.

One AI maxim says, "What we focus on expands." Time and attention on our flaws expands the flaws; time and attention on core strengths expands the strength.

Appreciative Inquiry helps create a shared vision of what is possible and engages people in working towards it. The attention is on the positive work of building the common vision, not on fixing problems. Yet problems get solved in the process of working toward shared aspirations.

Analyzing the "cause and cure" of problems too often entraps people in a spiral of blame and negativity that tears at the fiber of social capital and paralyzes efforts to change. AI solves problems by outgrowing them.

Carl Jung could have been speaking of appreciative inquiry when he said, "All the greatest and most important problems of life are fundamentally insoluble…They can never be solved, but only outgrown." Problems get solved along the way to pursuing a compelling vision.

Jung observed, "Some higher or wider interest appeared on the horizon and through this broadening of outlook the insoluble problem lost its urgency. It was not solved logically in its own terms, but faded when confronted with a new and stronger life urge."

Cooperrider noted four phases that support the development of a positive core: Discovery, Dream, Design, and Destiny.

Discovery
Identifying what gives life to the organization when it is most effective and capable.

Dream
Envisioning possibilities.

Design
Collaborating on the ideal of what ought to be.

Destiny
Creating the ideal daily through continual learning and adjustment. This phase is self-sustaining, leading to even greater strength and capacity.

How can you begin to use AI to strengthen and transform your organization? It all starts with conversation. Cooperrider advises, "Think of appreciative inquiry as a new conversation, as a search engine for the positive core of a system..."

Ask questions that are framed as unconditionally positive. For instance, rather than asking your team, "Why is morale so low?" ask, "When have you felt most satisfied and engaged in our work?"

As people share their stories, watch the enthusiasm grow and the core of your organization gain strength.

Linda DeArment

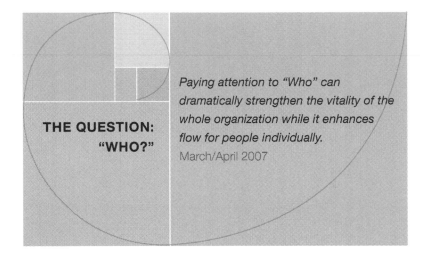

THE QUESTION: "WHO?"

Paying attention to "Who" can dramatically strengthen the vitality of the whole organization while it enhances flow for people individually.
March/April 2007

Who will do the work? What will they produce? These questions, if answered well, can engender flow, enthusiasm, vitality, and teamwork. If not well considered, they can deplete morale, increase turnover, and frustrate cooperation.

The key to working smarter (not harder) is to pay more attention to the question: *"Who?"*

We all have natural predispositions to the way we approach work. That predisposition often constitutes our best contribution to the overall success of a group. When people are using their best gifts in collaboration with others, the whole organization becomes more creative, productive, and vital.

We at Partners for Innovation have begun applying the insights of the GiftsCompass™ Inventory (GCI)—an online self-assessment—to optimize the inherent strength of teams. The GCI enables us to better align the natural gifts of individuals with their contribution to the team (see: www.giftscompass.com).

Generally, there are four primary approaches to work: *formulating, reflecting, associating,* and *producing.* Each of these approaches has a natural application in organizations. If a team is charged with producing a new product or service, for example, any phase of the process—conception, planning, or implementation—might need one or more of those four.

The conception stage might rely heavily on those inclined to use the *formulating* approach. They are often the ones with imaginative, systematic, big-picture orientations.

Planning might need those favoring the *producing* approach for it would likely involve developing and coordinating goals, schedules, and strategies.

The implementation phase might need those favoring the *associating* approach with their preference for working with people rather than data.

A *reflecting* approach might be needed at every important juncture to provide the creative, thought-provoking insight that insures that the work is consistent with the highest aspirations of the organization.

Paying attention to the question, "Who?" can dramatically strengthen the vitality of the whole organization while it enhances *flow* for people individually.

James Latimer

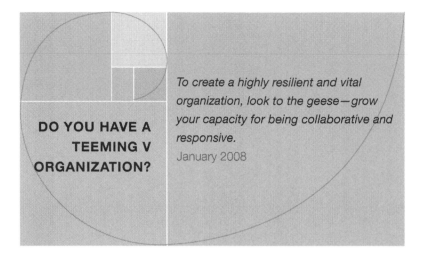

To create a highly resilient and vital organization, look to the geese—grow your capacity for being collaborative and responsive.

January 2008

We, at Partners for Innovation, refer to organizations that are resilient and vital as *Teeming V Organizations*, acknowledging that the V-shaped formation of geese provides a memorable metaphor for being highly responsive and collaborative. Four principles distinguish Teeming V Organizations:

Lead so that others do too.

The most effective leaders cultivate leadership in others. Resilient and vital organizations depend on *every* individual taking initiative and responsibility.

Promote the value of *individuals*.

When competent people are doing work they are passionate about, everything changes. Their enthusiasm and energy are contagious. Cooperative trust among those individuals forms the intangible, diverse fabric of social capital.

Build a responsive network.

Responsive organizations continually engage collaborative innovation. Organizations that successfully create a context for people to learn, think, and respond freely toward a common end, engender extraordinary results.

Find a mission that matters.

A mission that differentiates the unique *value* of the organization evokes deep commitment and clarifies a unifying purpose for diverse initiatives.

If you can insure that these four attributes are present, you are likely building a vital and resilient organization. These *Teeming V* attributes have been derived from years of research, writing, and onsite experience. They have been tested and confirmed in many organizational settings.

To create a highly resilient and vital organization, look to the geese—grow your capacity for being collaborative and responsive.

But what if we could distill the few basic principles of greatness that could apply to all organizations—irrespective of their tax status? That is what we have sought to accomplish with this article.

September 2008

BUILDING FORCES FOR GOOD TO GREAT

I recently attended a presentation by one of the authors of the newly released book, *Forces for Good: The Six Practices of High-Impact Nonprofits*. Like the books *Good to Great* and *Built to Last* that evaluate for-profit companies, the authors sought to find a few basic principles that differentiate the really vital and enduring nonprofit organizations.

All three books make valuable contributions to the literature on vital organizations. Each contains particularly insightful observations about "greatness."

But what if we could distill the few basic principles of greatness that could apply to *all* organizations—irrespective of their tax status? That is what we have sought to accomplish with this article. In reviewing all three books, we have identified three principles found in each.

Responsive Innovation

All three books emphasized the need for perpetual, responsive innovation. In *Built to Last,* they called it "Good enough never is" and "try a lot of stuff and keep what works;" in *Good to Great* it was the "flywheel of innovation;" in *Forces for Good*, it appeared as "mastering the art of adaptation."

All three of these valuable guides to building vital and enduring organizations advocated a process of perpetual learning, adapting, and innovating. It is the DNA of vital transformation—a network of motivated people empowered to produce change wherever and whenever change is needed.

But to create that DNA requires a different kind of leadership.

Inclusive Leaders

In *Forces for Good*, they called it "shared leadership;" in *Built to Last*, it was "clock building not time telling;" in *Good to Great* they coined a new term: "Level V."

In each case, they spoke of organization-centered leaders rather than ego-centered leaders—those who are intent on building inclusive dialogue, making collaborative decisions, sharing leadership with others, building people of strong character, keeping a view to the longer term vision, values, and systems of the organization.

A Mission that Matters

Like the geese that need a common destination, people in vital organizations need to understand the overriding value of what they do. They want to know that their lives count for something significant, that they can work for a purpose greater than their own self-interest.

In *Good to Great,* they called it the organization's "Hedgehog;" in *Built to Last*, it was "purpose beyond profits" and "Big Hairy Audacious Goals;" in *Forces for Good* it showed up as "inspiring evangelists." People are not automatons. If they are to create vital organizations they want to know that the organizations they serve are delivering real value.

Perpetual innovation, inclusive leadership and a mission that matters—if we can get those three right, we will be well on our way to building the great organizations that are themselves "forces for good."

———————————————

Social Capital: Follow Through

Capitalizing on Success

Change in organizations is often most easily accomplished by affirming what is already going well,
and then doing more of it. You could use the space below to note
the essays on social capital that highlight your current success and
also what more you might do to build on that success.

Essay Title	What else could be done?

Fixing Problems

While affirming and capitalizing on success may be the easiest way to grow collaborative genius, problems may also have to be addressed. You could use the space below to note essays that have highlighted impediments to growing collaborative genius, and what you might do to address them.

Essay Title	What could be done?

SOUL

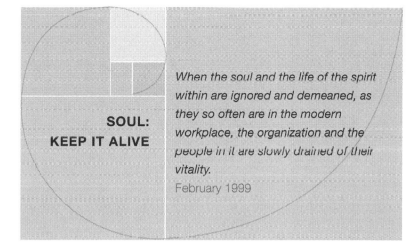

SOUL:
KEEP IT ALIVE

When the soul and the life of the spirit within are ignored and demeaned, as they so often are in the modern workplace, the organization and the people in it are slowly drained of their vitality.

February 1999

Shamans of the Navaho Tribe teach that people can become *de-spirited*. That is, they can lose touch, if they are not careful, with the source of spiritual guidance within them. When people become de-spirited, they become little more than a vacuous shell—a facade with nothing behind it.

The idea of inner spiritual guidance is also at the heart of western religious traditions. The Judaic-Christian traditions, dating back more than three thousand years, are rich with lessons of the influence of the unseen, but deeply felt, spirit.

This unseen, deeply felt, inner life was at the center of Carl Jung's model of psychology. He saw how our materialistic, outward-centered culture often runs roughshod over the inner life of the soul.

When the soul and the life of the spirit within are ignored and demeaned, as they so often are in the modern workplace, the organization and the people in it are slowly drained of their vitality.

Truly creative and collaborative groups depend on a lively inner life. The inner life of the soul must be honored as part of the culture of the organization. Without soul, what difference does it make if a group of people "gains the whole world." They will have experienced a chilling absence of spiritual life, without which they are "de-spirited"—just a hollow facade.

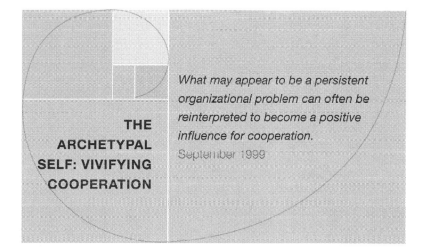

THE ARCHETYPAL SELF: VIVIFYING COOPERATION

What may appear to be a persistent organizational problem can often be reinterpreted to become a positive influence for cooperation.

September 1999

Artists intuit patterns and see images; scientists observe repetitions and create hypotheses. Jungian psychology has been gaining popular attention because it combines the artistic inclination to see patterns and images with the scientific rigor of empirical observation and creative hypothesizing.

By combining these seemingly antagonistic ways of viewing reality, Jung's approach provides a fresh point of view for approaching tricky and persistent organizational problems.

A key concept in this approach is Jung's notion of *archetypal patterns*—patterns of psychic energy that play into our daily lives, often without our being aware of them.

For Jung, the source and center of these patterns is the *Self*—a dynamically interactive pattern of perfected wholeness. The Self is not a religious concept, though it bears much similarity to religious symbolism from many traditions. One of Jung's contributions to the emerging field of psychology was linking this timeless religious experience with secular psychology.

The Self pervades human life in all dimensions, centering and ordering our lives at the deepest levels. Understanding the nature of this experience has profound consequences for developing cooperative groups.

With a common understanding of the Self and the attendant archetypal patterns, groups tend to build bonds that transcend superficial differences. What may appear to be a persistent organizational problem can often be reinterpreted to become a positive influence for cooperation.

The value of Jung's profound empirical inquiry into archetypal patterns is only just beginning to influence organizations. The value of that inquiry is surely destined to play a significant role in vivifying the way we work together.

Angelo Spoto

ROOTING OUR WORK IN THE DREAM OF GOD

If groups are to collaborate harmoniously and meaningfully—to connect purpose-to-purpose—then we must begin by rooting our work in the collective experience of our own souls, in the dream of God.

January 2000

The power to generate ideas—an awesome power—is too often taken for granted. We have built entire civilizations out of this simple potent capacity to generate an idea and act on it.

But history has shown that ideas can go astray. Even though we might wish otherwise, the ideas that can build a world of compassion do not always prevail; journalists remind us daily of that fact. If God does indeed have an ideal dream for the civilization we are to build here, it seems apparent that what we humans have created over the last five thousand years is out of step with that dream.

What is missing? How could we drift so far afield from a more ideal world? The missing element may well be God's dream itself, the presence of God and the images that issue from that intangible presence.

In his insightful book, *The God We Never Knew*, Marcus Borg talks about God's dream for the world, and the need to seek that dream in our work. It is a dream, Borg says, that is alive and in our midst, not held by some aloof Deity, but available to us minute-to-minute. It is a dream of heaven but also a dream of heaven on earth, right here among us and in this world.

Too often, we engage in generating ideas before fixing the direction and vision for those ideas from our collective experience of God's dream. In doing so, we divorce our conscious lives from the inner experience of our souls.

In the final analysis, if our work is not integrated with our souls, we are engaging in self-delusion. Our egos may get a boost from a new sense of power, but the gnawing two-thousand-year-old question remains: How do we profit if we gain the whole world but lose our souls in the process?

If groups are to collaborate harmoniously and meaningfully—to connect purpose-to-purpose—then we must begin by rooting our work in the collective experience of our own souls, *in the dream of God.*

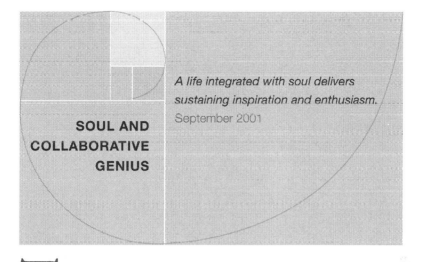

SOUL AND COLLABORATIVE GENIUS

A life integrated with soul delivers sustaining inspiration and enthusiasm.

September 2001

The soul plays an extraordinary role in the course of human development and is an integral element in our work lives. It cannot be hung at the door to our place of work, to be picked up again on our way out. We cannot separate ourselves from the life of the soul.

We each seem to carry a dream of life within us. We have aspirations for the life we would ideally like to live. The soul speaks to us daily this way. We get pictures and images, whispers and intuitions of a more complete and full life. We are drawn to that life.

When the groups we join resonate with that vision, we gain energy. To awaken collaborative genius, these dreams, passions, and visions must also be awakened.

There is a heroic inner journey underway for each of us—a journey to our own potential. The call to allow our full potential to emerge, to allow the deeper self to find expression in life, is always with us. It is a journey of passages that requires effort, struggle, and movement to attain the next threshold.

As Joseph Campbell *(The Hero With a Thousand Faces)* wrote, "But whether small or great, and no matter what the stage or grade of life, the call rings up the curtain, always, on a mystery of transfiguration—a rite, or moment, of spiritual passage, which, when complete, amounts to a dying and a birth. The familiar life horizon has been outgrown; the old concepts, ideals, and emotional patterns no longer fit; the time for the passing of a threshold is at hand."

When we deny the soul's journey and attempt to compartmentalize our lives in some narrow and obedient social pigeonhole, when we avoid this call to growth, we suffer *disintegration*. We separate our conscious lives from an integrated life with the soul. Our integrity with this inner call is askew.

Writers from fields as diverse as physics and psychology have noted the necessity of living an integrated life. As physicist David Bohm *(Wholeness and the Implicate Order)* wrote, "All of this indicates that man has sensed always that wholeness or integrity is an absolute necessity to make life worth living."

From Jungian analyst Thomas Moore *(The Care of the Soul)* we hear, "The great malady of the twentieth century, implicated in all of our troubles and affecting us individually and socially, is 'loss of soul.' When soul is neglected, it doesn't just go away; it appears symptomatically in obsession, addiction, violence and loss of meaning."

The place where we work, no matter what the purpose of the enterprise, can stimulate this integration with soul, or it can suppress it. When work brings the soul to life, the whole and replete person shows up. A life integrated with soul delivers sustaining inspiration and enthusiasm.

Matthew Fox *(The Reinvention of Work)* has said that we all yearn to make a contribution in life, "Every heart longs to be part of something big and sacred." The work that allows people to more freely express their own heroic journeys—that engages that inner urge to make a meaningful contribution—also engenders collaborative genius.

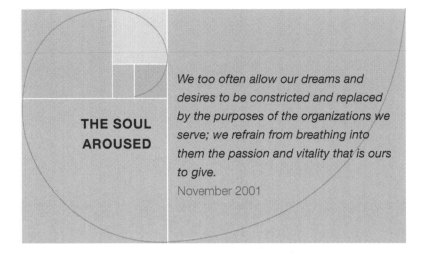

THE SOUL AROUSED

We too often allow our dreams and desires to be constricted and replaced by the purposes of the organizations we serve; we refrain from breathing into them the passion and vitality that is ours to give.

November 2001

In the middle of the road of my life
I awoke in a dark wood
Where the true way was wholly lost.

Dante

Too many have lost their way in corporate America. Surveys have shown that more than 50% of workers are dissatisfied with their jobs. The most dangerous time in a man's life is at nine o'clock on Monday morning when a heart attack is most likely to occur. The other very dangerous time is just after retirement from work, when most fatal illnesses occur. One death is caused by the strain of carrying the façade of a soulless life, the other by the stress of losing that façade.

What is soul? Soul is beyond definition. It cannot be touched, but can be felt; it cannot be seen, but is self-evident to inner vision; it cannot be heard; yet we are ever prodded by its still, small voice. It is like the tiny mustard seed: It can grow so large that birds of the air build their nests in its branches, or it can remain indiscernibly small if the seed falls on barren soil. The shaping of soul is the ultimate human endeavor.

We cannot tangibly grasp soul, but we can feel the palpable anxiety and vacant pit in our stomachs that a life without soul engenders. As Joseph Campbell observed: if we do not come to know the deeper mythic resonances that make up our lives, those mythic resonances will simply rise up and take us.

Those mythic resonances call each of us to unique lives. They are at the heart of our unique identities and purposes in life. Our educational systems, institutions, and corporations may suggest that we should all think and look alike. But such dogma will kill the soul within us all.

Diversity is the essence of soul. The organization that usurps our unique purpose and destiny suffocates the soul. Those who artificially conform to other people's standards at the expense of their own are like Oscar Wilde's acquaintance who, "…has no enemies but is intensely disliked by all his friends."

We too often allow our dreams and desires to be constricted and replaced by the purposes of the organizations we serve; we refrain from breathing into them the passion and vitality that is ours to give. Then we wonder why those organizations seem to have such a stranglehold on our lives. "Tomorrow," we say. "I'll make a change tomorrow, but in the meantime, I'll make do." Then ten years go by and we find ourselves awakening in a dark wood where "the true way is wholly lost."

What if organizations could be the places where our individual passions find expression, where the soul can live and breathe? What if they could be highly innovative places where the inherent creativity of people's lives steps outside their prescribed job descriptions, where the full capability of the unique individual is brought to bear for the benefit of the whole?

What would it be like if the complexity and vitality of an organization were born of the passion, vision, and imagination of its members, instead of constricted by a mechanistic organizational chart? What if we developed new metaphors for organizations that started with soul and individual passion, rather than trying to stuff that passion into a prescribed job description?

What would it be like if we could create organizations where the soul was aroused, rather than stifled? To have organizations where 100% of the people love their work, this is precisely what we must create. The soul will not have it any other way.

To die inside, is to rob our outside life of any sense of arrival from that interior. Our work is to make ourselves visible in the world. This is the soul's individual journey, and the soul would much rather fail at its own life than succeed at someone else's.

David Whyte

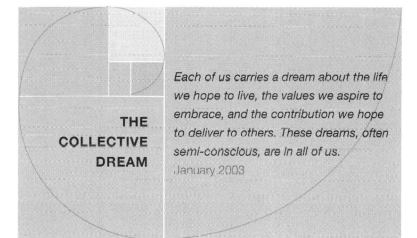

THE COLLECTIVE DREAM

Each of us carries a dream about the life we hope to live, the values we aspire to embrace, and the contribution we hope to deliver to others. These dreams, often semi-conscious, are in all of us.

January 2003

Several of our previous articles have referred to the need to bring the soul to life in organizations, for integrating the soul is essential to a healthy organization, as well as a healthy personal life.

But how, specifically, do you accomplish that? Certainly mystics, psychologists, religionists and philosophers have offered sage counsel about integrating soul in the life of the individual. But few have addressed the question of bringing the soul to life in organizations. In 2003 our Innovation Tips articles will focus on that important inquiry. This article, on The Collective Dream, is the first in that series.

Each of us carries a dream about the life we hope to live, the values we aspire to embrace, and the contribution we hope to deliver to others. These dreams, often semi-conscious, are in all of us. They pervade our lives like the air we breathe, always with us, always calling us forth into a new life.

When we live life sequestered from this pervasive dream, we separate ourselves from our souls. Living life separated from soul has disturbing consequences. As Thomas Moore insightfully observed, "When soul is neglected, it doesn't just go away; it appears symptomatically in obsession, addiction, violence, and loss of meaning."

When an organization respects and cultivates the dreams carried in the collective soul of its members, it taps deep and enduring spiritual sources of inspiration and energy. When people's work lives are congruent with the aspirations of the soul, they are richly connected to the unseen spiritual rhythms that guide and direct their lives.

But the organization that tries to impose its own culture of self-interest on the collective dream of its people will repress those guiding spiritual rhythms. Homogeneous cultures that impose a one-size-fits all cultural hegemony on people will drain vital energies and engender conflict.

To cultivate and secure the collective dream, look for ways to channel people where their passions and enthusiasm take them; defer to the autonomous initiatives and aspirations of small energized groups; relax the managerial controls that keep people shackled to an inflexible bureaucracy—give people the freedom to give expression to their own enthusiasm and energy. Let them live.

Order has little to do with control. In the passions and enthusiasm that people bring to work, there exists an unseen implicit order—the order of the soul. Leaders who step aside from their controlling attitudes and constricting personal agendas will allow the dynamic order of the collective dream to emerge.

They will bring the soul to life.

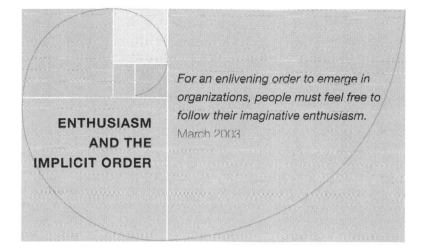

For an enlivening order to emerge in organizations, people must feel free to follow their imaginative enthusiasm.
March 2003

I n setting up strict, highly defined control systems in organizations, we fragment and disable the collaborative genius of the whole. An implicit order—a rich and enlivening order beneath the surface of things—directs and animates the vitality of the organization. Our imposed control mechanisms too often interfere with that more invigorating order of life.

We can find that order by paying attention to *enthusiasm*. Enthusiasm, energy, interests, and imagination all guide us to the implicit order. We *notice* our imaginative enthusiasm; we do not produce it. It is of the soul, and the soul is beyond our control.

For an enlivening order to emerge in organizations, people must feel free to follow their imaginative enthusiasm. When the enthusiasm of the soul is alive, it brings an enduring vitality to the entire enterprise.

People won't pursue their enthusiasm when managerial rules and controls hold them in harness. The more rules imposed on them, the less enthusiasm they will bring to the work; the more controls, the less imagination. Both enthusiasm and imagination are vital to a thriving on collaborative genius.

An organization's deepest value is not in its fragmented and disenfranchised parts. The deepest value lies in passionate and connected diversity. Promoting diversity does not always look orderly, yet it will produce far more human energy than any system of compartmentalized controls.

People do not get passionate about conforming to other people's standards and expectations. They grow passionate about expressing their own ideas, their own enthusiasm, and their own creative response.

As diversity born of ideas and enthusiasm emerges, it gives shape to a new fluid and dynamic order. It gives expression to a living implicit order that is so much more effective, enlivening, and responsive than any managerial control systems could ever hope to be.

When we put material gain ahead of deeply held values of integrity, we commit the folly of the ages. We multiply our possessions, perhaps, but lose touch with our own souls.

April 2003

Our principle of separation between church and state seems to have also imprinted our cultures at work: We have too often built a chasm between soul-centered values and organizational management.

A chasm between spiritual loyalties and selfish purposes is at the root of corporate malfeasance recently in the news and the decisions of top management to "cook the books" for personal gain—witness the fiascoes at Enron, Global Crossing, and World-Com.

When we put material gain ahead of deeply held values of integrity, we commit the folly of the ages. We multiply our possessions, perhaps, but lose touch with our own souls. When the accepted business ethic degenerates to one of profits first and values second, the soul of the organization is in jeopardy.

What is the value of increasing material wealth if we fail to develop an invaluable life? How does it profit the world to generate steep profits if, in so doing, we generate shallow characters?

Corporations that worship at the altar of profits displace much-needed attention to values. In the long term, these corporations often fail to sustain the profitability they once held so dear. Ironically, those organizations that do attend to values seem also to produce the most enduring success.

Amazon, for example, is steadily emerging as a retail giant, not because they have their eye predominantly on the bottom line but because they don't. They are building a culture that prides itself on delivering the highest customer satisfaction ratings in the industry.

In the end, the Enrons of the world, those that seem to put short-term profits and capitalized value ahead of all else, fail at the very objectives they had set out to accomplish, for they leave the soul of the organization behind.

The soul sponsors humility, imagination, and an authentic passion for life. When we bring these attributes forth in an organization, we have enlivened an enthusiasm for the work that cannot be accessed through purely material objectives.

For real dialogue to occur there can be no hidden agendas. People must bring honesty and candor to the conversation and listen fully without judgment or distraction.
May 2003

Few people personify the value and purpose of dialogue better than the influential Jewish theologian and scholar, Martin Buber. Many remember him best for his book, *I and Thou*, the title of which succinctly expresses the essential message of the book: When we regard another as "Thou" rather than as "it," we have entered into a sacred relationship of dialogue.

Buber was attracted to Eastern and Christian mysticism and to Hasidic Judaism because of their emphasis on a spiritual union with God. He admired the Hasidic commitment to creating a society that truly lived by faith in God—a commitment Buber regarded as "the greatest phenomenon in the history of the Spirit."

Real dialogue, when the I-Thou attitude is present, is the centerpiece of enlivened community. For Buber, the relationships formed in dialogue generate holiness and justice in the world. People honor and respect one another; they set their own personal agendas aside to truly listen and attend to another. In these liberating and evolving conversations of daily life, the very spirit of the living God seems present, for "Every Thou is a glimpse through to the eternal Thou."

By contrast, I-it relationships stifle community. They are manipulative and calculated for personal gain. I-it conversations imprison the soul and suffocate the Spirit; they engender mistrust and deception.

True dialogue requires a high level of authenticity—"essential courage" as Buber called it. For real dialogue to occur there can be no hidden agendas. People must bring honesty and candor to the conversation and listen fully without judgment or distraction. A life of dialogue generates passion and reverence.

As Buber reminds us all—every individual and every organization—dialogue is at the very heart of community. Where dialogue thrives, the soul truly comes to life.

———————

BRINGING THE SOUL TO LIFE: LIBERATING CREATIVITY

. . . we must vigilantly avoid excessive control if we are to liberate creative thinking. The life of the soul, and of the organization, depend upon it.

June 2003

Creative imagination is an expression of soul. Where creativity thrives, the soul is alive and well. When the soul is brought to life in an organization, creative imagination naturally arrives with it. If creativity is stifled, so too is the soul.

Creative ideas are easier to stifle than to stimulate. Too often organizations have found the magic formula for killing creativity: Control people rather than liberate them.

Organizational control can take many forms. One of them is controlling decision-making. If people feel they have no say in the key decisions, they may feel a sense of powerlessness that can drain their creativity. The organizations most effective in bringing creativity to life give people a voice in decision-making—they give them a legitimate stake in the success of the enterprise.

Criticism is another form of control. Tentative ideas have to thrive if creativity is to flourish. Elegant and profound ideas seldom hatch full-grown; they must be nurtured and cultivated to come to maturity. Early criticism will stifle the creative process.

It has been said that the degree to which people will use their creative imagination is inversely proportional to the amount of punishment they will receive for using it. Criticism is one form of punishment, and it will control and deplete the creative output of the whole organization.

Political manipulation is explicitly controlling. If people with organizational power appear secretive or politically manipulative, they will generate an atmosphere of mistrust and uncertainty. Creativity requires open and candid conversation; creativity wanes in a culture thick with mistrust.

Bureaucracy is heavy with control. If any new or bright idea must be subject to the review and approval of cumbersome layers of management, it will die an early death. People need to feel that they can own the germinating process of developing their ideas.

Some organizations do more to kill creativity than to cultivate it. Managers too often see their own work as necessarily controlling the work of others. But we must vigilantly avoid excessive control if we are to liberate creative thinking. The life of the soul, and of the organization, depend upon it.

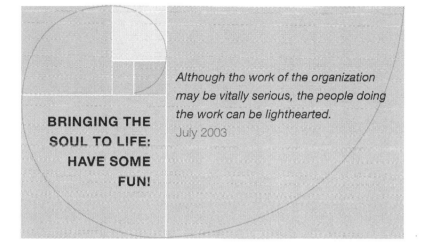

BRINGING THE SOUL TO LIFE: HAVE SOME FUN!

Although the work of the organization may be vitally serious, the people doing the work can be lighthearted.

July 2003

W here ideas are being born, people are having fun. The more fun, the more creativity—this seems to be axiomatic. Humor paves the way for the flow of ideas; it greases the skids for an unselfconscious ride on the delightful track of creative thinking.

The negative axiom also applies: the absence of fun will kill ideas. Yet, too many organizations seem incorrigibly determined to become deadly serious. When people take themselves too seriously, they suppress the soul and kill creative thinking; they isolate people from one another with departmental silos and hierarchical barriers. Stiff hierarchies suppress the festivity. People can hardly relax when they risk judgment from an almighty boss.

Organizations invested in prestige, pride, power, or position will reap the artificial rewards of affected self-importance.

But the soul does not beget self-importance; rather, it engenders humility, appreciation for others, and inclusive humor. Although the work of the organization may be vitally serious, the people doing the work can be lighthearted.

The fishmongers of Seattle that converted the boring work of selling fish into perpetual play transformed a little known operation into one that has become virtually world famous. People come to watch their antics as a form of lunchtime entertainment. Fun has not adversely impacted their business. As these retailers of fish will freely tell you, while they are having the time of their lives, they are also selling a lot of fish.

IDEO, now one of the most prominent industrial design firms in the world, still creates offices where people feel free to have fun; to hang their bicycles on systems of pulleys from the trusses over their unorthodox work spaces; to play practical jokes on anyone and everyone in the company; to collaborate irrepressibly and spontaneously in generating some of the most elegant and inventive product designs in the history of the industrialized world.

The groups that are really enjoying themselves frequently have a blow out good time; they celebrate together often. Humor, fun, a sense of equality, valuing people for their contribution not their title—these are the attributes of an organization having fun.

If you want to know whether the soul has been brought to life in an organization, look at people's faces. Are they smiling? Are they enjoying themselves? A simple measure of the degree to which the soul has been brought to life is simply this: Are people having enough fun?

TRUST THE UNDERCURRENT OF CHANGE

The bold and audacious experience of anticipating the next possibility, the next open door, the next quantum leap to more fulfilling possibilities is where life is lived in the very sinew of the soul.
March 2004

Innovation awaits us all, and it is frightening. We are beckoned, in our personal lives and in our organizations, to move on through the next open door, to make that quantum leap to the next level of new possibilities, but the leap always seems treacherous.

If we only knew how truly safe it is. Change is the natural order of life itself. In this universe, we will be strangers in a stranger land if we cannot adapt to change.

We are swept, in our organizations and our lives, by an undercurrent of purpose toward the next, more fulfilling way of life. We create trouble for ourselves when we get tangled up in resistance and control—avoiding the newer and more fulfilling only because it is unfamiliar.

Resisting that undercurrent is like a swimmer fighting the strong current of a river just to stay in one place. It actually takes more energy for him to stay put than to swim with the natural flow of the river.

The flow of perpetual innovation can actually be more restful and is virtually always more energizing than staying put. Every organization, every individual is challenged to respond to changing conditions. Those that refuse to change can grind themselves down with useless anxiety and misspent energy as they cling to the status quo.

Unless we are willing to disown that which is no longer serviceable, we cannot freely take ownership of the enthralling future that awaits us. To the degree that fear or attachment to "turf" keep us bound up in anxiety over change, we deprive ourselves of the heightened vitality ahead.

When we finally arrive, after a long strenuous struggle of resistance, kicking and screaming into our intended destiny, we wonder what all the fuss was about.

The bold and audacious experience of anticipating the next possibility, the next open door, the next quantum leap to more fulfilling possibilities is where life is lived in the very sinew of the soul. In our organizations and in our personal lives, we must learn to trust the undercurrents of change, for that change is much safer than we know.

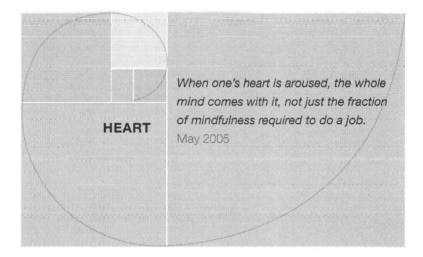

When one's heart is aroused, the whole mind comes with it, not just the fraction of mindfulness required to do a job.
May 2005

HEART

Cultivating the heart of an organization requires far more than doing a good job with performance appraisals, job descriptions, rewards, and punishments. One's heartfelt commitment to work transcends the rational mechanisms created to motivate and control, for, as Pascal reminds us, the heart has reasons that reason cannot know.

Great Groups, those groups that gel and produce extraordinary accomplishments, would find insulting the standard management mechanisms considered as "best practices." Those who commit themselves—heart, mind and soul—to the work of Great Groups do so to feel fully alive, not to get high marks from their supervisor.

All of us, as Matthew Fox has repeatedly written, want to feel that we are part of something big and sacred. Our work can be big and sacred if our hearts are in it. When our heart is aroused, our whole mind comes with it, not just the fraction of mindfulness required to do a job.

People who do what brings them joy discover a special passion that transcends the mundane and seemingly senseless work of daily toil. They tap a passion that runs deep to their core. Teilhard de Chardin, the acclaimed Catholic theologian, regarded joy as the "infallible sign of the presence of God."

Who among us knows what "heart" or "joy" really is? But we know enough to recognize that we want to feel fully alive; we want to feel the lightning of pure joy running through our veins. It behooves us all, as Joseph Campbell advised, to follow our own bliss. When we do, we discover a passion for living that we desperately want to sustain.

That joy for us all can be sustained in organizations where the heart is alive and well, where people are valued individually and engaged in bringing their full and heartfelt contribution to the organization. This is the transcendent task of leadership, not to supervise and control, but to enable people to bring their heartfelt commitment to the work—to discover and sustain what brings them joy.

"Organizations can keep searching for new ties that bind us to them—new incentives, rewards, punishments," wrote Margaret Wheatley, the organizational development consultant and author who looks to nature for her inspirations about organizational management. "But organizations could accomplish so much more if they relied on the passion evoked when we connect to others, purpose to purpose. So many of us want to be more. So many of us hunger to discover who we might become together."

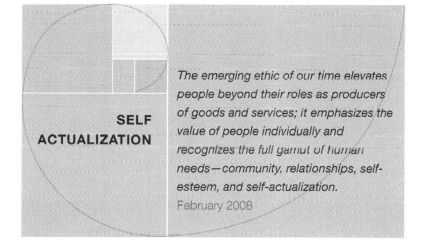

SELF ACTUALIZATION

The emerging ethic of our time elevates people beyond their roles as producers of goods and services; it emphasizes the value of people individually and recognizes the full gamut of human needs—community, relationships, self-esteem, and self-actualization.

February 2008

We live at a time when organizational success will increasingly depend on the value of creative individuals acting as change agents. The emerging ethic of our time elevates people beyond their roles as producers of goods and services; it emphasizes the value of people *individually* and recognizes the full gamut of human needs—community, relationships, self-esteem, and self-actualization.

Yet the residual management ethic in some organizations is still derived from the industrial age: Frederick Taylor's mechanical view of people at work. Organizations that rely on coercion, control, and strict hierarchies will suppress the new ethic. With that suppression, they will also suppress their own vitality in a world increasingly dependent on the creative contribution of individuals.

The new ethic transcends Taylor's theory; it acknowledges people's *whole* lives—personal commitments, roles, passions, interests, aspirations, and spiritual depth. Its focus is the *self-actualization* of the individual.

Practical reasons abound for valuing people holistically. Research has shown that people will take on more responsibility, work with greater enthusiasm, and be more productive. They will experience less stress, take fewer sick days, and stay with the organization longer.

Creating a context for self-actualization will require new practices and new a new management mentality. Every tried-and-true "best practice" will need to be reexamined. Some have already begun to push the envelope of best practices.

One example is the Brazilian manufacturing company Semco, where they apply a democratic approach to organizational management. (See *Maverick: The Success Story Behind the World's Most Unusual Workplace* by Ricardo Semler.) Poet David Whyte has poignantly written about the need to bring the soul and full individuality to life in organizations. (See *The Heart Aroused: Poetry and the Preservation of Soul in Corporate America.)*

They, along with many others, herald the new organizational ethic of our time, an ethic that values and promotes the unique identities, diverse lives, and complex needs of *individuals.*

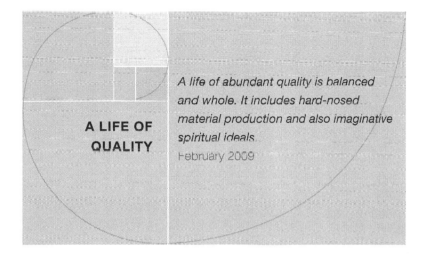

A LIFE OF QUALITY

A life of abundant quality is balanced and whole. It includes hard-nosed material production and also imaginative spiritual ideals.

February 2009

An American economist recently remarked that we might never again enjoy our current quality of life in this country. This sounds like dismal news.

Yet, we should remember that compared to the quality of life for the rest of the world, middle America has lived comparatively like kings and queens of old. 50% of the world's population suffers from malnutrition and less than 1% has had the benefit of a college education.

We constitute just 5% of the world's population, yet environmentalists tell us that we are generating about 25% of the world's waste. We have polluted more of the free air per capita than any other nation state. Symptoms of a profligate life erupt in other statistics: we have more violent crime, more road rage, and more people living in steel cages per capita than any other democracy in the world.

Now, at a time when our lifestyle may be abruptly constrained, we would do well to rethink the term "quality of life." We have the opportunity, amid paroxysms of economic turmoil and rampant fear of loss, to discover a *life of quality* that transcends old definitions.

Assessing life's quality through measures of material gain is insufficient. It is a one-sided bias that can result in more harm than health—both for individuals and for organizations.

A life of abundant quality is balanced and whole. It includes hard-nosed material production and also imaginative spiritual ideals. It consists of solitary intellectual pursuits and also interdependent relationships in community. These seeming opposites are woven together as a life of rich quality.

Quality, by definition, is not measured quantitatively. Yet that has been our cultural bent. The income level, the size of the house, the sticker price of the car, the prestige of the job—these have been the typical measures of the "quality" of our lives. These dashboard measures of material gain can help to gauge a few of the aspects of life's quality, but we need to monitor the dashboard gauges of other forms of quality as well.

We must also consider: Who has benefited from the life we have lived? How have we left the world better than we found it? What poetry has moved our soul this week? What books have altered our understanding of the world? To how many people can we honestly say, "I love you?" How much money have we given away to people or causes that we believe in?

An unbalanced, overly materialistic life engenders neurosis—whether for the individual, the organization or the culture. It has been too truly said that, "We have taller buildings but shorter tempers, fancier houses but broken homes, more conveniences but less time, more medicine but less wellness, steep profits and shallow relationships…We have learned how to make a living, but not a life."

The workplace is not just for work. It is a place of community where people may continue to pursue one of the preeminent purposes of life—to develop a life of abundant quality. In that pursuit, organizations become more vital and resilient.

Soul: Follow Through

Capitalizing on Success

Change in organizations is often most easily accomplished by affirming what is already going well, and then doing more of it. You could use the space below to note the essays on soul that highlight your current success and also what more you might do to build on that success.

Essay Title	What else could be done?

Fixing Problems

While affirming and capitalizing on success may be the easiest way to grow collaborative genius, problems may also have to be addressed. You could use the space below to note essays that have highlighted impediments to growing collaborative genius, and what you might do to address them.

Essay Title	What could be done?

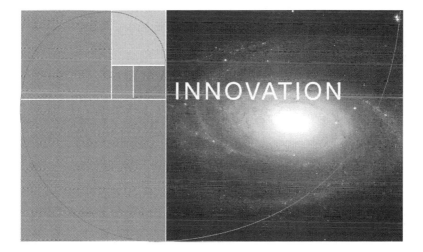

INNOVATION

THE MISSION: INNOVATING FOR A PURPOSE

Innovation simply comes more easily within the context of purpose. Creativity is paradoxically more difficult to achieve when there are no constraining boundaries.

January 1999

For organizations to be effective at innovation, it is helpful to have a clear and cogent mission. Creativity is paradoxically more difficult to achieve when there are *no* constraining boundaries. The creative impulse is strongest in response to a need rather than when exercised simply for the sake of being creative.

How do you clarify an organization's mission in terms that will help to produce innovative thinking?

The mission should express the operational value delivered to a constituency.

It should articulate what the organization *does* specifically to deliver value. For example, for a hospital to say, "We are in the business of providing excellent regional medical facilities," is less clear than saying, "We provide comfort, compassion, and care for the sick."

Providing medical facilities is not the value being delivered. People do not want medical facilities for their own sake. They want attentive and professional care when they are not well. Providing medical facilities is a necessary component of the mission, but it is not the mission itself.

Neither was "providing buggy whips" the mission at the turn of the century when automobiles were replacing carriages. Any mission that is stated in terms of products delivered rather than value delivered is likely missing the purposeful value of the organization.

When the mission is stated in clear terms that emphasize the operational value being delivered, people more readily see how their innovations contribute to achieving the organization's purposes.

The mission should be simple and memorable.

The mission that attempts to be meaningful to everyone and rambles on for half a page, piling on ideas, values, insights, concerns and priorities from all corners of the organization in an effort to build consensus and to be inclusive, will be meaningful to *no one*.

Any statement of mission ought to be subject to the one-breath rule—if you can't say it in one breath, it is too long. If the mission is not memorable, then *ipso facto* it will be forgotten.

The ultimate purpose of the organization's mission is to mobilize resources for getting the *right* things done and for innovating in ways that support the organization's mission. Innovation comes more easily within a clear context of *purpose*.

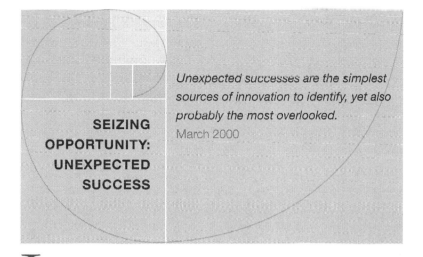

SEIZING OPPORTUNITY: UNEXPECTED SUCCESS

Unexpected successes are the simplest sources of innovation to identify, yet also probably the most overlooked.
March 2000

Innovation often arises from paying attention to events in the day-to-day operations of the organization. Though there are many fertile events that can lead to innovation, perhaps the richest is also the simplest to identify and the easiest to implement: *unexpected success.*

Unexpected successes can occur anywhere in an organization's operating environment. Regardless of where those unexpected successes are found, they can provide a basis for simple and sometimes profoundly effective innovation.

To illustrate, IBM originally developed the computer for scientists; they believed that targeted group was the optimal market for a machine that could do complex calculations at a fast pace. As they executed their marketing plan for that market, they noticed something unusual happening—businesses were also showing interest their machines. The interest from the business community was completely unexpected. Their computing processes were not nearly as complex as those required for science

They could have ignored the unexpected interest from a market they had not anticipated. They could have kept their full attention on their strategic plan, but IBM responded, adapted their product, and developed a strategy for probing the business market. The business market grew to be their most profitable market.

The IBM example helps to illustrate the importance of responding to *unexpected* success. Some organizations get so focused on the superhighway of their strategic plan that they ignore the various unexpected successes occurring casually along the side of the road.

Unexpected successes are the simplest sources of innovation to identify, yet also probably the most overlooked. They are too often regarded as interesting anomalies *on the way* to achieving targeted objectives. The lesson for organizations is simply to remain flexible and responsive to these events when they occur. Serendipitous unexpected successes are often packed with bountiful potential, sometimes more than the targeted objectives of a strategic plan.

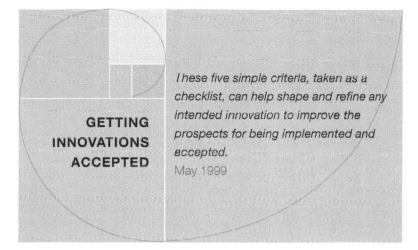

These five simple criteria, taken as a checklist, can help shape and refine any intended innovation to improve the prospects for being implemented and accepted.

May 1999

The creative work of developing innovations is not enough. If the innovations are not accepted by the market or an intended constituency all the creative work will have been for nothing. In his groundbreaking work, *The Diffusion of Innovation,* Everett Rogers identified five key factors for increasing the acceptance of innovations.

Perceived Advantage

Innovation needs to be perceived as being superior in some significant way to whatever it is replacing. Unless the innovation is *perceived* as superior to an existing alternative, it will likely be rejected.

Familiar

Innovation ought to feel like part of a continuum of familiar values or experiences. Innovations that are too strange or too inconsistent with cultural norms will not likely be accepted.

Simple

An innovation needs to be a fairly simple change to be adopted quickly. If the change is seen as overly complicated, hard to understand, or too difficult to learn, people will resist adopting it.

Easy to Try

If an innovation can be sampled without risk, it will be more readily accepted. People need to have the hands-on experience of using it and experimenting with it to feel comfortable with making a change.

Tangible Results

If the successful results of implementing an innovation are readily apparent, the innovation is more likely to be adopted. People need to see tangible results to be convinced of an innovation's advantages.

These five simple criteria, taken as a checklist, can help shape and refine any intended innovation to improve the prospects of being *accepted* successfully.

2009 Addendum:

Malcolm Gladwell's important book, *The Tipping Point*, is also worth mentioning on this subject. He notes the likelihood of adoption for a new trend or innovation is also dependent on key people in social networks. Successful adoption is linked to two types of people—*mavens* and *connectors*. The mavens are the knowledge-based experts who can confirm and communicate that a trend or innovation is worthy of adoption. The connectors are those typically more gregarious people who are connected to many others and who informally promote the innovation.

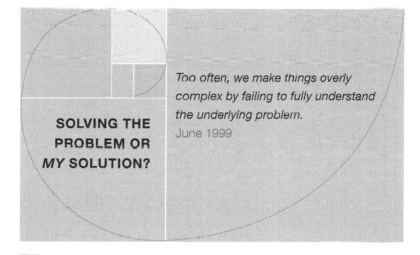

SOLVING THE PROBLEM OR MY SOLUTION?

Too often, we make things overly complex by failing to fully understand the underlying problem.

June 1999

In your organization, are you solving the problem or your *solution* to the problem? The two are not always easy to separate. Too often, we make things overly complex by failing to fully understand the underlying problem. The following two stories, perhaps both anecdotal, will help to illustrate this conundrum.

A property manager needed to deal with tenant complaints about a long wait for elevators. She was presented with three alternatives, all costly: increase the speed of existing elevators; move the elevators; or install new ones. Her solution: none of them.

Perceiving that the real problem was not the speed of the elevators but the tenants' *dissatisfaction while waiting,* she installed mirrors in the lobby. The mirrors gave people something to focus on while waiting (themselves). The complaints ceased.

An investment banker was at the pier of a small coastal Mexican village when a small boat with just one fisherman docked. Inside the small boat were a few yellowfin tuna. The banker complimented the fisherman on the quality of his fish and asked how long it took to catch them.

The fisherman replied, "Only a little while." The investment banker then asked why he didn't stay out longer and catch more fish. The fisherman said he had enough to support his family's immediate needs. The banker then asked what he did with the rest of his time.

The fisherman said, "I sleep late, play with my children, fish a little, take a siesta with my wife, Maria, stroll into the village each evening where I sip wine and play guitar with my amigos. I have a full and busy life."

The banker scoffed, "I am a Harvard MBA and could help you. You should spend more time fishing and with the proceeds, buy a bigger boat. With the proceeds from the bigger boat you could buy many boats, eventually owning a whole a fleet of fishing boats. You would sell directly to the processor, eliminating the middleman, eventually opening your own cannery. You would control the product, processing, and distribution. You would leave this small coastal fishing village and move to Mexico City, then L.A., and finally to New York where you would run everything."

The fisherman asked, "But, how long will all this take?" "15-20 years." "But what then?" The banker laughed: "Oh! That's the best part! You would announce an IPO, sell your stock and become very rich. You would make millions!" "Millions? Then what?"

"Then you would move to a small coastal fishing village where you could sleep late, fish a little, play with your kids, take a siesta with your wife, stroll to the village in the evenings where you could sip wine and play your guitar with your amigos!"

Whenever considering an organizational problem, we could all remember these stories and ask, "Am I solving the problem, or *my* solution to the problem?"

Is there anything about your operation that is a source of complaint for anyone? When you pinpoint those complaints, you will have identified a rich source of creative innovation.

July 1999

Innovation is often a process of resolving some nagging problem. It starts with dissonance, with difficulty, with chaos, with toe stubbing, or abject failure—something that needs fixing.

It is a process, as Schumpeter described it, of *creative destruction*. Something is usually changed, modified, or destroyed for innovation to occur. Some thing, some approach, or some paradigm must be altered for a new and better way to emerge.

How can you find these sources of innovation, these approaches that need a touch of creative destruction? *Complaints* are one readily available source. If you can find out what people are complaining about and why, you will have identified a fertile source of innovation.

What are people complaining about in your organization? What bothers your customers or constituency, distribution network, or suppliers? Is there anything about your operation that is a source of complaint for anyone? When you pinpoint those complaints, you will have identified a rich source of creative innovation.

One of the most creative customer response cards we've seen comes from Susan Sargent Design, Textiles:

> Please **COMPLAIN.** Thanks for you order! We want everything to go $P E R F E C T L Y!$ If the order was late. Or wrong. Or if any of the goods are damaged in the slightest. Or if you're just having a lousy day and want to unload on someone...Call our customer care hotline.

What are people complaining about in and around your organization? Do you have a way to uncover those complaints? Mining for nagging complaints can unearth the raw materials for precious innovations.

———————————

BASIC ELEMENTS OF SUCCESSFUL INNOVATION

Small, tightly focused incremental changes grounded in hands-on experience are the stuff of successful innovation. Staying firmly connected to these three characteristics can help to build an attentive, innovative organization.

August 1999

Though innovation may sound glamorous and exciting, it is often simply a matter of doing everyday work differently. Many of the most successful innovations are not monumental or earthshaking changes. Rather, they often consist of small, targeted changes that usually possess these three characteristics:

Grounded

Successful innovations are often grounded in immediate opportunity. They are usually a response to current needs, securely built on direct experience with that need; they are usually built from gritty hands-on experience.

Focused

They often constitute just a subtle change in the way things are done. Seldom are innovations so monumental or breathtaking that they rock the whole system or market. They often impact a very limited segment of a market, product, or process. They grow in complexity and impact as they mature.

Small

Really effective innovations often start small. Sometimes they are just little pilot projects started in a garage, on a coffee table, or in the bathtub of a dorm room. Some of the greatest success stories of the last twenty years started small this way—Microsoft, Cisco, and Dell to name a few. The innovative founders of these companies were just playing with focused ideas to solve immediate needs.

Small, tightly focused incremental changes grounded in hands-on experience are the stuff of successful innovation. Staying firmly connected to these three characteristics can help to build an attentive, innovative organization.

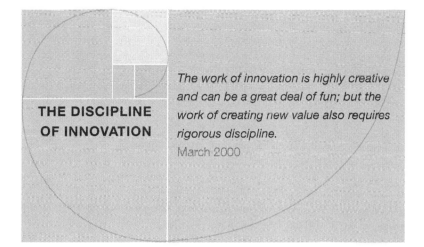

THE DISCIPLINE OF INNOVATION

The work of innovation is highly creative and can be a great deal of fun; but the work of creating new value also requires rigorous discipline.

March 2000

Innovation can produce *novelty*—something that is new and different, but not especially valuable. In a highly innovative environment, we might all be tempted to produce the cool and creative, just for the sake of producing something new and innovative.

One of the most innovative companies in the world, Apple computer, may have fallen into the novelty trap when they produced the "Cube" computer. It was elegant, simple, new, different, but did it add *value?*

That is the key question for any change, any new product or service, any modification in the way things are being done. *Does it create value?*

The seven windows of opportunity described in Peter Drucker's book, *Innovation and Entrepreneurship*, are vital reference points for identifying opportunities to add value. If an innovation is not born from one of these windows of opportunity, it will not likely create much value.

The first three of these seven windows tend to generate the garden-variety innovations where the value to be created is clear.

Window 1: The Unexpected

The first window is the window of the *unexpected* event. It presents the opportunities for innovation that are the easiest to seize—though ironically also the most overlooked. Both unexpected successes and failures are included in this window.

Window 2: Incongruities

The second window highlights the issues related to products, services, and operating modes where something needs adjustment. Something may be occurring that seems incongruous—it is happening but it seems that it ought not be; *or* it is not occurring though it seems that it ought to be.

Window 3: Process Needs

The third window highlights those aspects of a process that needs to be fixed. They are the weak links in chain of events that perpetually seem to fail.

Taking periodic inventory of an organization's products, operations, and strategies through these three windows can produce abundant opportunities to create value.

There are also four other windows that address the bigger picture strategic opportunities like changes in market structure or demographics. They too ought to be part of the discipline of innovation, though their opportunities to add value are often longer term and more capital intensive.

The work of innovation is highly creative and can be a great deal of fun; but the work of creating new value also requires rigorous discipline. Using these windows of opportunity as reference points helps to answer the all-important question for any change: does it create value?

We would all do well to pay attention to the disruptive incongruities around us — those symptoms that denote significant structural changes in our operating environments.

June 2000

We may often assume that if we persist in ongoing improvement, if we listen to our customers or our constituencies, if we continually improve our service or our products, we will be successful and thrive. And this is the very mantra that brings great companies to their knees and sometimes destroys whole industries.

Though constant innovation and improvement are important, they can also blind us to the significant incongruities in our operating environment that, if not fully understood, can bring the demise of the organization. These significant incongruities are often symptoms of disruptive innovations—those new approaches to delivering products or services that often accompany major and lasting market changes.

The classic example of products that were destined to fail, and with them whole companies and even an entire industry, were buggy whips around the turn of the century. A disruptive innovation had been introduced that would put virtually all the buggy whip manufacturers out of business. With our hindsight of one hundred years, we know that disruptive innovation was the automobile. But living in those times, when travel by horse-drawn carriage was simply the way people *always* traveled, the introduction of the "horseless carriage" probably didn't appear to be much of a threat.

Automobiles were too expensive for common people and they were notoriously plagued with mechanical failures. Yet the disruptive innovation of the automobile, though crude at first, did prevail, and virtually eliminated companies devoted to horse-drawn travel. Continually improving the manufacture of buggy whips would not protect them from the disruptive innovation of automobiles.

We too live in an age when there are new disruptive innovations being introduced at every turn. In every walk of life, in every industry, dramatic and often sudden change is afoot that can undermine the very survival of an industry. Disruptive innovation occurs in advanced technology, where the rate of change is astounding; it occurs in the medical industry, where market changes are upending traditional modes of delivering care; it has occurred in hospice care, where advanced medical treatments are impinging on the palliative care formerly reserved for hospice; it has occurred among religious institutions that have been the moral backbone of society.

We would all do well to pay attention to the disruptive incongruities around us—those symptoms that denote significant structural changes in our operating environments. It is no longer enough just to pay close attention to the customer and to encourage constant improvement. It now behooves us to pay attention to what is amiss, to the disruptive innovations that may have a dramatic impact on the very survival of the organizations we serve.

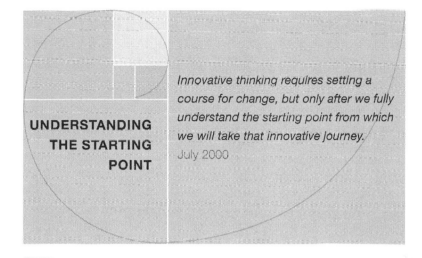

During our days as poor undergraduate students in Kentucky, my friends and I sometimes entertained ourselves by exploring rural roads to see what we might find. As you would expect, on some of these journeys we became hopelessly lost. On one such occasion, we stopped to ask an old man working on a fence near his barn how we could get back to the city. He listened intently, paused before answering and then said prosaically, "Well, if I were going there, I wouldn't start from here."

Over the years, his answer has provided us with much amusement. With the passing of time, however, I have also come to see the wisdom in this simple statement. Often, when faced with a problem, our response is to set a course for change. What we sometimes neglect, however, is the time needed to fully understand our starting point, the current state of affairs that is producing the perceived need for change. Without a thorough understanding of where we are, we may try to get to our destination by setting a course from the wrong starting point.

In the 1950s, shipping by boat was too slow. Everyone agreed that changes needed to be made and that the ultimate goal was to deliver products to their destination more quickly. For years, the response to this challenge was to improve the ships that carried the cargo. Engineers found ways to build faster vessels carrying larger loads with smaller crews.

What the industry leaders had failed to understand was that the problem was not slow moving ships; it was a bottleneck at the docks where the ships were unloaded. Increasing the speed of the ships just made the bottleneck worse. As my college friends and I had done, these shipping companies may have had the correct destination in mind, but they were setting off from the wrong starting point.

Social scientists have often suggested that, in order to fully understand a situation, we must be willing to become "strangers in a familiar world"; in other words, we must not assume that we really know the environment in which we operate. Innovative thinking requires setting a course for change, but only after we fully understand the *starting point* from which we will take that innovative journey.

Marvin Moore

Strategic planning may be an excellent planning process, but most organizations can no longer afford to just plan; they must also strategically innovate.

August 2000

In the former days of traditional business models, when the world was changing more slowly, when people could more accurately predict growth, and when they could look to the past to anticipate the future, strategic planning was the classic approach to guiding an organization's development.

But few of us live in that world anymore. We now live in a world of constant change where the past is no longer necessarily prologue, where we often do not know where the next dramatic change will be coming from. In our new and unpredictable world, organizations that want to thrive must be nimble, proactive, inventive, inquisitive, and inclusive.

In his characteristically blunt style, Tom Peters has said of this new world, "If you think you know what is going on, if you feel like you have a pretty good understanding of what is happening around you, then you are *desperately out of touch*."

In an environment of rapid, ongoing change, the process of strategic planning has inherent flaws. Few strategic planning processes produce real strategic innovation, a means of capitalizing on new opportunities in formation. The mindset that generates strategic planning tends to produce programming rather than innovation, the predictable and conventional rather than the bold and creative.

Strategic planning assumes that the future is fairly predictable, that current or past circumstances can be relied upon to anticipate future events. That underlying assumption is much less reliable now.

Strategic planning is often limited to a relatively small group of managers or board members. The rest of the people who are feeling the day-to-day pulse of change are often omitted from the process. They may be asked later to align themselves with the results of planning, only elevating their feelings of disenfranchisement.

In environments of perpetual change where organizations need to adapt to unexpected events, the entire living network of the organization needs to be engaged to make sense of change in the making.

Organizations need responsive and flexible strategies that capitalize on opportunities as they begin to take shape and challenge current conventional thinking. They need to engage the inquisitive and creative contributions of the whole organization in strategic innovation that responds to emerging opportunities and threats.

In today's rapidly changing world, organizations must constantly innovate—change and adapt. Strategic planning may be an excellent planning process, but most organizations can no longer afford to just plan; they must also *strategically innovate.*

IMPLICIT RULES: THE HOBGOBLIN OF INNOVATION

We often need to first identify the implicit rule or pattern that has us buried in a problem, that took us "down" into feeling that the problem could not be solved, and find a way to break that implicit rule.

September 2000

Implicit rules are unspoken habits of mind that often direct our behavior and the way we think about challenges—*usually unconsciously*. When problems have us wrapped up, when they seem insoluble, some implicit rule usually has us trapped in the problem.

Consistency breeds implicit rules. Obedience to consistency is a powerful inhibitor. No matter how innovative we may think we are, we all, somewhere in our lives, are blindly following some pattern of consistency without being fully aware of it. We are all occasionally subject to the "hobgoblin of little minds" as Emerson referred to foolish consistency, in some aspect of our lives.

Certainly, consistency is necessary for much of the world to function. You wouldn't want to wake up every morning to learn that someone had changed the rules of the road and altered the meaning of traffic lights and signals. But when consistency breeds implicit rules that obstruct a solution, they become our prisons.

To solve the problem, we have to stage a jailbreak. As Picasso understood, "The act of creation is first of all an act of destruction." The pre-Socratic Greek philosopher, Heraclitus, perhaps unwittingly provided guidance for breaking free of implicit rules when he said, "The way down is also the way up."

We often need to first identify the implicit rule or pattern that has us buried in a problem, that took us "down" into feeling that the problem could not be solved, and find a way to break that implicit rule. Then we can often find the innovative solution that allows us to transcend the problem and find our way up and out of it.

Consider how many significant innovations have been born by breaking implicit rules. Beethoven broke the rules about how to conduct a symphony. Napoleon broke the rules for conducting a military campaign. Copernicus broke the rules about the earth's station in the universe. Leonardo da Vinci broke virtually all the rules all the time and gave birth to thoughts and inventions—helicopters and submarines—that would not materialize for hundreds of years.

What implicit rules may be retarding the innovative growth of your organization? Identify them and reduce their hold. When you do, you will find your way to a more enlivening, successful, and creative way to work.

PAYING ATTENTION IN THE AGE OF DISCONTINUITY

Learning to live with the seeming chaos of accelerating change will try our patience, challenge our core values and stress the very fabric of our civilization. Yet in the chaos of such change, there is also possibility.

March 2001

We live in an age of unprecedented change. Many of us are hoping that it will settle out soon, that all of this disruptive change will slow down so that life can get back to normal. It won't. The rapidity of change will accelerate, causing emotional, social, and economic disruption across all levels of society. As Dorothy noted, we are simply not in Kansas any more.

Some have referred to this period of rampant change as the age of "discontinuity"—the abrupt passing of one way and the sudden commencement of another. Every industry, every business, every institution, every way of life will be affected by these unsettling discontinuities.

We will no longer be able to rely on the past to help us anticipate the future; rather, we must now use new ways of understanding what is ahead of us, and we must also develop new ways to respond.

Purposeful innovation in this new age will be needed for the well-being of every business, organization, and institution. Knowing how and when to effectively innovate will be essential to successfully respond to the change occurring all around us. Opportunity for innovation occurs in at least two forms:

Continuous Improvement

The simplest, most conventional form of innovation is what the Japanese call *Kaizen*—continuous improvement. It is the easiest to understand and the easiest to access. Continuous improvement simply means adding value to existing products, processes, services, and practices. Those improvements often occur in response to some basic questions: Where have we had an unexpected success or failure? What seems amiss or in need of fixing? Where are the weak points in the flow of our work?

"New Concept" Innovation

More difficult to manage, though rich with opportunity, are "new concept" innovations: fiber optic cable in lieu of copper wire, disposable diapers in lieu of cloth, aluminum cans in lieu of glass bottles, cash management accounts in lieu of savings accounts, credit cards in lieu of cash or check, or solid state electronics in lieu of vacuum tubes.

New concept innovation can plague every organization at the top of its game. Powerful blue-chip companies have been brought to their knees by such innovations, not the least of which have been IBM, Xerox, Sears, and NCR.

Learning to live with the seeming chaos of accelerating change will try our patience, challenge our core values, and stress the very fabric of our civilization. Yet in the chaos of such change, there is also possibility. With every advance and every change, new opportunity is born for those who are paying attention.

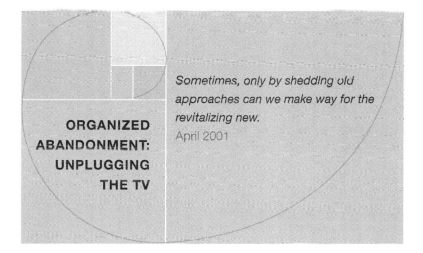

Sometimes, only by shedding old approaches can we make way for the revitalizing new.
April 2001

Sometimes, what we choose to unlearn is as important as what we learn. Letting go is hard for us all; we all tend to resist change. We get comfortable with the way things are and our natural tendency is to preserve the status quo. But we have only so much time and so many resources. If we are to pursue that which contributes to growth, greater effectiveness, and a more significant product or service, we must often unlearn—*abandon*—old practices.

Jim Collins (co-author of *Built to Last*) shared a personal story at a national conference of religious leaders to make that point. He had set a goal of reading and absorbing two new books per week, wanting to add value to his consulting practice as well as to his personal development. He equipped his study with all the right stuff—a comfortable reading chair, desk, bookshelves, and reading light.

But the initiative failed in the early going. Instead of spending the time reading, as he intended, he found himself slipping back into the old habit, the old ritual, of turning on the TV just to see what was on. Once the TV was on, he was hooked. His decision to read two books per week was sabotaged by his old habit of watching TV.

When he realized what was going on, he *unplugged* the TV (and later gave it away). Only then could he make the time for his new, more personally profitable commitment.

Similarly, the highly innovative organization regularly puts every practice, every market, every distribution channel, every customer or client, and every product on trial for its life. The question that must continually be asked is this: *If we were not doing this already, would we choose to do it now?*

If the answer is no, then whatever it is may need to be discontinued. If it is stunting the growth of the organization, or obstructing the development of something more promising, then it may need to be abandoned. Sometimes, only by shedding old approaches can we make way for the revitalizing new.

What is old habit, outmoded process, or vestigial, long-held practice that is holding your organization back from a better way? Identify it and "unplug it" and you will have cleared the way for a new and better approach to organizational effectiveness.

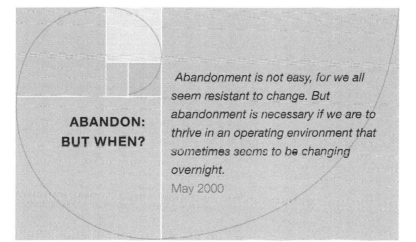

ABANDON: BUT WHEN?

Abandonment is not easy, for we all seem resistant to change. But abandonment is necessary if we are to thrive in an operating environment that sometimes seems to be changing overnight.

May 2000

We know that highly innovative organizations must systematically abandon practices or products that are no longer serviceable. But how do we know when to abandon a product or mode of operation?

In his book, *Management Practices for the 21st Century*, Peter Drucker has offered three general criteria.

It still has a few good years left.

When it is generally agreed that a product, service or operational practice "still has a few good years left," it is probably time to abandon it. Drucker points out that we too often grossly overestimate the life that is truly left in a dying operation and grossly underestimate the organizational energy required to sustain it. Attempting to garner a few more years too frequently drains the energy and intelligence of some of the most productive people in the organization; it saps their creative and enlivening energies.

The assets are fully written off.

Sometimes assets are viewed from a one-sided accounting perspective. Just because an asset has been written off does not make it any more productive. From an economic perspective, there are only sunk costs. The key management question for an asset is this: "What will it produce?" If the asset is only being retained because it has been fully depreciated, it is likely time to reconsider its usefulness.

The old is stunting the development of the new.

An entrenched traditional practice is a frequent saboteur of innovation. When old processes are stunting the development of newer, more effective ones, it is time to abandon the old. This is hard and often complicated, for a company's livelihood may be inextricably tied to old processes.

The development of the Saturn automobile is a prime example: The development of Saturn was starved by attempts to modernize Oldsmobile and Buick plants, even though Saturn was experiencing ascending success and the more traditional brands were on the decline.

Michael Dell built one of the most successful businesses of the last decade around a shift in the way computers could be made and distributed. The old approach assumed that the computer was made first, and then sold. Dell inverted that assumption, selling first and then making the computer. Dell also created a new distribution system. His company sold directly to consumers and "custom-made" each computer to the individual user's specifications. Other computer manufacturers were loath to abandon their established distribution systems, for their ties to middlemen were too well entrenched.

There will be times when a traditional practice, service, or product simply must be abandoned to retain the ability to compete, or to more effectively serve a client/customer base. Abandonment is not easy, for we all seem resistant to change. But abandonment is necessary if we are to thrive in an operating environment that sometimes seems to be changing overnight.

Entrepreneurs are often thought of as risk takers—they bet the farm; they put it all on red. Yet research suggests that successful entrepreneurs are often not big risk takers. In fact, they do all they can to contain risk.

June 2001

Innovation—creating new value—always carries some measure of risk. If the innovation is a significant one, the risk may also be quite significant. Market tests, surveys, and focus groups may not accurately assess the introduction of something truly new. A new concept must often be introduced to prospective users and tried before reliable information about it can be learned and applied.

When Ford introduced their new Edsel in the 1950's, after conducting exhaustive market research, they were confident that they were creating a great success. It flopped.

When Chrysler introduced the LeBaron convertible, they built a prototype and Lee Iacocca drove it back and forth to work for a while. When people stopped him on the highway wanting to know where he bought that "great car", they put it in production. It was a runaway success.

Ford relied on market research; Chrysler built a prototype. Ford jumped in with both feet; Chrysler put their toes in the water. Both took on great risk; but one took a bath while the other took a load off its balance sheet.

Entrepreneurs are often thought of as risk takers—they bet the farm; they put it all on red. Yet research suggests that successful entrepreneurs are often *not* big risk takers. In fact, they do all they can to contain risk.

One way to contain risk, as Chrysler demonstrated through the introduction of the LeBaron convertible, is through *prototypes*—pilot projects used to test a new idea. Focus groups, surveys, personal interviews, and systems thinking all have their important place. But for the introduction of a truly new idea, there are few substitutes for prototypes.

A prototype can quickly pinpoint the successes and trouble spots in a new idea; it can test the idea without betting the farm or restructuring the whole organization. Out of these often playful or rough pilot projects, seriously effective new processes, products, and approaches emerge.

Prototypes test the water before committing huge organizational resources. They create the space for creative thinking to occur before the project becomes an unwieldy behemoth.

Many of the world's most successful innovators thrive on prototypes: Hewlett Packard, 3M, and IDEO to name a few. Companies less inclined to use prototypes tend to fall behind. Their inability to successfully test ideas with prototypes has been a root cause of their decline in market prominence.

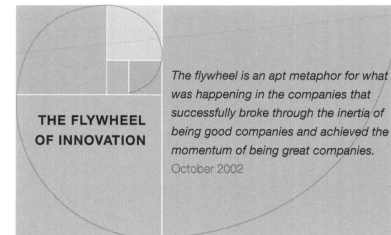

THE FLYWHEEL OF INNOVATION

The flywheel is an apt metaphor for what was happening in the companies that successfully broke through the inertia of being good companies and achieved the momentum of being great companies.
October 2002

It is no secret that large scale organizational change initiatives often fail. An abrupt overhaul of an organization too often creates more frustration than value, generating dissension, annoyance, resentment, and even chaos, rather than enhanced order. However, structural change may be necessary for the organization to remain vital and effective.

How, then, ought those organizations make those necessary and important changes? Jim Collins' recent book, *Good to Great*, offers some clues. He and his team of researchers studied the extraordinarily successful organizations that effectively transformed themselves from good to great, as measured by their profitability and capitalized value.

Collins observed that they did not usually attain their success through major overhauls; rather, their success occurred at a more gradual pace. The innovations that occurred often happened in small doses. Small successes spawned other success; change and success motivated more of the same. The purposeful change occurred like a "flywheel" of innovation.

Picture a heavy flywheel, thirty feet in diameter, two feet thick, made of steel, and mounted on an axle. Imagine that your task is to get that flywheel moving as fast and for as long as possible. Each time you push, the flywheel moves a bit, then a bit more, each time a bit faster. Each push gradually increases the momentum until at a certain point the flywheel's momentum carries itself. You are pushing no harder than you were the first time, yet the pushing seems to now easily increase the speed of the flywheel. The inertia that kept it at rest has been broken; its own momentum now keeps it turning.

The flywheel is an apt metaphor for what was happening in the companies that successfully broke through the inertia of being good companies and achieved the momentum of being great companies. There were no wrenching revolutions, no overnight metamorphoses, no single, profound innovations, and no grand master plans. They transformed themselves one small step, one small innovation at a time. Push by push, turn by turn, they moved the flywheel of incremental innovation until their momentum generated sustained, even spectacular, results.

The flywheel of innovation can catch on in an organization, but getting it moving, overcoming the inertia and resistance to change, takes time. Yet the time spent cultivating small, successful innovations anywhere and everywhere in the organization is well worth the effort, for the flywheel of innovation will roll on to perpetually change the organization for the better.

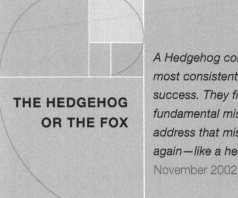

A Hedgehog companies are those that most consistently attain unusual success. They find their one fundamental mission in the world and address that mission over and over again—like a hedgehog.

November 2002

" T he fox knows many things, but the hedgehog knows one big thing." So wrote the ancient Greek poet Archilochus.

The hedgehog knows one defense, to curl into a compact prickly ball, a strategy that consistently defeats the cunning fox, which has many stratagems. The hedgehog is simple; the fox is complicated. The hedgehog does one thing and does it exceptionally well. The fox does many things, craftily.

Speaking of the hedgehog and the fox as psychological types, Isaiah Berlin noted, "For there exists a great chasm between those, on one side, who relate everything to a single central vision…a single, universal, organizing principle in terms of which alone all that they are and say has significance—and, on the other side, those who pursue many ends, often unrelated and even contradictory."

Which is better for organizations, to be a hedgehog or a fox? The truth is that organizations, like individuals, have been successful as both. No one would argue that General Electric—a very talented fox—has not been successful in many of its diverse ventures.

Yet, Jim Collins has noted, in his recent book, *Good to Great*, that the hedgehog companies are those that most consistently attain unusual success. They find their one fundamental mission in the world and address that mission over and over again—like a hedgehog.

Their "Hedgehog Concept" as he calls it, refers to that one, central value proposition that the organization can offer better than any other. The value proposition does not just fall out of the sky. It is usually the outcome of much rumination and soul-searching.

Dialogue about a proposed Hedgehog Concept must survive the scrutiny of three types of inquiries:

Passion

Does it elicit passion for the work? Is it worth working hard to attain? Will people be genuinely enthusiastic about it?

Competence

Does it build on core competencies? What can the organization do better than any other? Is it consistent with the organization's experience of unexpected success?

Value

Does it deliver a sought-after value that can fuel the economic engines of the organization? What does the constituency value? Why will people choose the organization's value proposition over the competition?

Walgreens and Abbott Laboratories are examples of companies that have applied their own Hedgehog Concepts to attain exceptional success. Walgreens beat the economic results of GE, Coca-Cola, and Merck with one simple idea: offer the most convenient drugstores and maximize sales per customer visit. Recognizing that it could no longer be a premier pharmaceutical company, Abbot Laboratories turned its attention to delivering products that reduce the cost of health care.

Each of these companies attained superb financial results. The Hedgehog, or the Fox? The hedgehog knows one strategy; the fox knows many. Yet the Hedgehog frustrates the fox every time.

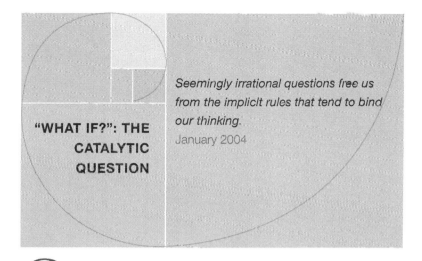

"WHAT IF?": THE CATALYTIC QUESTION

Seemingly irrational questions free us from the implicit rules that tend to bind our thinking.

January 2004

Creativity isn't that difficult, really, as long as we ask the right questions. If the question we ask is, "How have we always done it?" then we will kill creativity every time. But if the question we ask begins with the two simple words "what if," we lay the groundwork for creativity and for sometimes profoundly important and effective innovation.

The words "what if" are stepping-stones from what *is* to what is *possible*. Creative people, hard-wired to look for new possibilities, tend to rely on these stones almost unconsciously. Those two words initiate the indispensable catalytic questions that frequently lead to new, simple, elegant, profound, creative approaches to virtually everything. Creative people may rely on them unconsciously, but all of us can learn to make them part of our conscious dialogue.

Sometimes catalytic questions seem absurd, but if pursued, lead to remarkable accomplishments. The question "What if we could put a man on the moon in ten years?" initiated the astonishing NASA program under the Kennedy administration that *did* put a man on the moon. "What if planes were invisible?" led to the nearly incredible development of stealth aircraft that are virtually invisible to radar.

Seemingly irrational questions free us from the implicit rules that tend to bind our thinking. Once freed from those unconscious constraints, we can free-associate to other, more practical ideas. It is much easier to bring an idea back to a practical application than it is to free ideas from the mental box of practicality that constrains them.

When groups use this sort of wide-open thinking, everyone involved has to exercise some patience. Absurd "What if?" questions nearly always arouse precipitous judgment. It is certainly easy to pass judgment on the seemingly ridiculous. It is much easier to criticize than to compose.

But it is so much more *fun* to take the imaginative excursions that open new perspectives and free us from the standards and norms of traditional practices.

The Dutch seem to have a lot of fun thinking this way, even at the level of city government. I love one of their more recent creative ideas. The use of the public urinals must have been getting out of hand, for they were in need of increased janitorial attention. One can only imagine the sort of "What if?" questions they must have generated to arrive at their innovative, simple idea: They painted a fly at the bottom of the urinal. This seemed to solve their problem; it turned a normal bodily function into a sport.

There is no telling where that one catalytic question will lead. "What if?" It put a man on the moon and effortlessly maintained the public men's rooms in a city in Holland. *What if* you used it more in your organization?

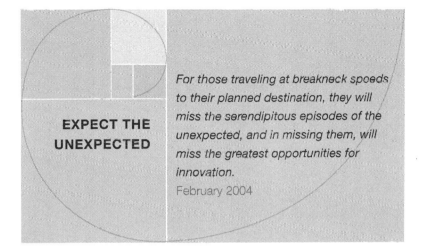

For those traveling at breakneck speeds to their planned destination, they will miss the serendipitous episodes of the unexpected, and in missing them, will miss the greatest opportunities for innovation.

February 2004

In a world of big boardrooms, gigantic plans, mighty strategies, and powerful tactics, the words of the ancient Greek sage Heraclitus speak softly to us through the millennia—*expect the unexpected*.

So sweet do the words of that enigmatic philosopher sound. His fragmented wisdom speaks to us today like some oracle in the wind. It whispers as a reminder that we are *not* in control of our future.

How different is the timbre of his words from those left on the mammoth pedestal of Shelley's ancient mythic king: "Gaze on my words ye mighty, and despair!"

Heraclitus suggests that we are not so great. Rather, he calls us to the task and sacred journey of paying attention to what he called the *Logos*—the subtle, profound, life-giving reason of life itself. "Expect the unexpected," reminds us that we may make our strategic plans and set our goals and priorities, but events are not under our control. Our hubris may be our undoing.

In this age of discontinuity where only one thing is certain—that nothing is certain—we must look again to the ancient wisdom of those who knew life more intimately.

We are here to respond, not to direct, nor to control. Our role is to serve. If we are to serve well, our plans and strategies must always be subject to what is happening around us and to how those we serve are responding to our work.

The greatest opportunities for both success and service lie in the *unexpected*. If we are embedded too deeply in our controlling plans and strategies, we will miss these opportunities every time. The unexpected occurs along the side of the highway of great plans and strategies.

For those traveling at breakneck speeds to their planned destination, they will miss the serendipitous episodes of the unexpected, and in missing them, will miss the greatest opportunities for innovation.

Strategic *innovation* is the road to thriving success. Strategic innovation requires listening to our friend and ancient sage: *expect the unexpected*. The side roads and byways of unexpected successes and failures are, ironically, the surest way to the success we seek.

The superhighways of control will often swiftly deliver us to the same empire-building destination that awaited Shelly's mythic king: "Amid the decay of that colossal wreck, boundless and bare, the lone and level sands stretch far away."

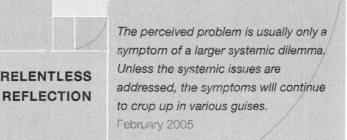

The perceived problem is usually only a symptom of a larger systemic dilemma. Unless the systemic issues are addressed, the symptoms will continue to crop up in various guises.

February 2005

I t is sublime, it is profound, it is simple, and it is one of the most powerful habits that any person or organization can pursue. Yet it is commonly suppressed in organizations. *Relentless reflection* is the productive habit that engenders continual improvement and sustained results.

As the extraordinarily successful companies in *Good to Great* illustrate, continual learning and incremental improvement generate the greatest long-term value. Relentless reflection leading to persistent innovation is their common hallmark.

Reflection is an indispensable practice in collaborative innovation. Without it, the entire system of thoughtful decision making breaks down. Solutions do not address the underlying problems; instead they address the symptoms. Thorough reflective thinking uncovers the problems behind the problem—the underlying causes that are the true source of dysfunction. Only with thorough reflection can those critical underlying issues be brought to light.

The perceived problem is usually only a symptom of a larger systemic dilemma. Unless the systemic issues are addressed, the symptoms will continue to crop up in various guises. Relentless reflection fleshes out root causes while it generates renewed enthusiasm for organizational problem solving.

But reflection is most often avoided in our take-charge and get-it-done-now culture. We are too prone to see a problem and fire off a solution, too quick to react—to make the singular executive decision. This reactive impulse to immediate action will drive any good company into the ground.

Managers struggling too hard to produce quick results tend to put out fires, find quick fixes, or apply proverbial band-aids. They work harder, not smarter. Their focus is on short-term results rather than building a productive culture. They count on numbers rather than the collaborative genius of people. With this misplaced focus, the whole organization is put in jeopardy.

Half-baked solutions will always create more problems than they solve. Failing to consider the full dimensions of a problem leads inevitably to poor decisions. Along the way, as people are disenfranchised by faulty executive decisions, the social capital of the culture wears thin.

If organizations are to achieve the substantial results attained by the companies featured in *Good to Great*, hasty decision-making must be replaced with the far more effective practice of relentless reflection.

IMPLEMENT QUICKLY

Design patiently and deliberately, but implement quickly. That is the formula that will build energy, enthusiasm, ownership and commitment as it builds a more vital and productive organization.
March 2005

J ust as hasty decisions can short circuit productive reflection, so, too, can unnecessary procrastination. Both wear down the productive social capital of the culture, and with that erosion, the ability to make well-considered decisions.

The model for sound decision-making is very simple—learn, talk, and then create. Groups that use that model will typically arrive at more productive and beneficial solutions than those that do not. But the patient and reflective search inherent in that model is not an excuse to unnecessarily delay action.

Carefully considering issues is an integral element of the thinking process that has made companies like Toyota great. Reflective and generative dialogue can elicit full and robust perspectives while they build ownership and commitment. But if careful consideration is just used as an excuse to indecisively stall action, it will deplete commitment and ownership.

Once an issue has been fully considered and the best of several alternative solutions has been generated, it is time to *act* and everyone knows it. To do otherwise diminishes the significance of the people who participated in decision-making.

The learn-talk-create model assumes that the solution will be implemented quickly. The time for careful deliberation occurs during the process of making sense of issues and formulating solutions. No decision ought to be hastily shaped. But once the decision, design, or solution is formulated, it must be implemented.

The patient process of finding the right solution often builds a reservoir of anticipation and energy. To delay empties that reservoir and undermines trust. Design patiently and deliberately, but implement quickly. That is the formula that will build energy, enthusiasm, ownership, and commitment as it builds a more vital and productive organization.

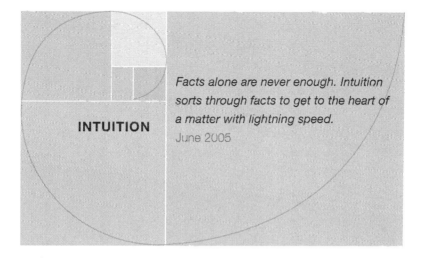

INTUITION

Facts alone are never enough. Intuition sorts through facts to get to the heart of a matter with lightning speed.
June 2005

A conceptual leap, a strong hunch, instantaneous knowing, gut feel, creative synthesizing, visionary imagination—how shall we describe intuition? Intuition is not ranked among the five cognitive senses, yet intuition can be the "sixth sense" that makes sense of the other five.

"State your reasons!" "Define your terms." "Tell me why you think that." "Back that up with hard facts." These are the conventional oppressors of intuitive thinking. Hard-nosed decision-making has little patience for the soft and imprecise guidance of intuition.

Yet the guidance of intuition must not be overlooked. Intuitive thinking often provides access to insights that are unattainable through conventional reasoning. Intuition, in one fell swoop, delivers solutions that step-by-step logic would never have seen.

When the inspiration of the intuitive vision arrives, we would do well to heed it. Though we cannot account for the sources of intuition, the historical list of those who pursued these intuitive understandings is long.

From Einstein, to Bach, to Dante, to Picasso, intuitive visions, epiphanies, hunches and leaps have delivered some of the most profound breakthroughs in science, music, literature, and art. But what does intuition have to do with the practical business of managing an organization?

Everything.

Intuition sorts through the never-ending stream of facts to deliver invaluable insights that can guide decision-making. Facts alone are never enough. Intuition sorts through facts to get to the heart of a matter with lightning speed.

Intuition delivers the visions and epiphanies that enliven organizations with the anticipation of more promising futures. As the Psalmist observed, without vision, the people (and organizations) perish.

Intuition is forever scanning, like subliminal radar, the cognitive dissonance that leads to productive and often powerful change.

We know so little about intuition. It cannot be touched, smelled, tasted, seen, or heard. Yet intuition is often the perceptive source of guidance that can lead our organizations to greatness.

CATALYTIC LEARNING

When we remain mindful of the information derived from the full range of experience—intuitive hunches, data, coworkers, clients, customers, stakeholders—we begin an invigorating cycle of productive change.

July/August 2005

Catalytic learning makes a difference; it is purposeful and focused. The aim is always the same—*innovation*. Its clear and specific purpose is to add value—to create more robust organizations that deliver greater value to their constituencies. It is a form of experiential learning that produces continual improvement. Catalytic learning starts simply with *being mindful*.

Peter Drucker (*Innovation and Entrepreneurship*) has built a framework for mindfulness—seven discreet "windows" of opportunity. Monitoring the cues and clues of experience through those windows delivers important information about needed change.

When we remain mindful of the information derived from the full range of experience—intuitive hunches, data, coworkers, clients, customers, stakeholders—we begin an invigorating cycle of productive change. Being fully mindful is a tireless sentinel's duty; the more sentinels the better.

Monitoring cues and clues can be one of the most important functions of a board of directors. A board brings the objective overview that is often lost by those entrenched in operational details. Boards may also bring the discerning experience and knowledge that can *make sense* of information.

Making sense of information is also critical to catalytic learning, for it fills out the relative importance and meaning of the partial cues and clues. The great mistake is to learn a fact and take immediate action.

Taking time to reflect and view any issue from diverse perspectives is a critical component of quality decision-making. If omitted, decisions are more likely to be half-baked—inadequately addressing the full underlying need.

Once information is understood from various perspectives and its relative importance evaluated, catalytic learning turns to *creative problem solving*. The creative thinking required to generate purposeful innovation is a key element in the cycle of catalytic learning. Creative thinking occurs best in nonjudgmental settings where fresh ideas can be uncritically heard and considered.

As innovations are generated, they are tested through experience and the cycle of learning repeats itself. Catalytic learning started with mindfulness and ends with mindfulness, for purposeful change, too, must be subject to reflective scrutiny.

The full cycle of catalytic learning requires diligence and attention. Once in motion, the cycle becomes a spiral of continual improvement that relentlessly generates an increasingly robust organization.

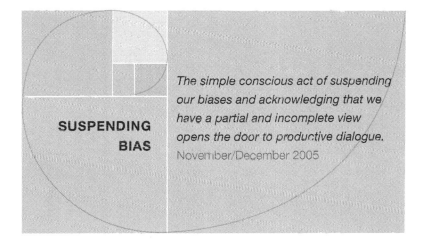

SUSPENDING BIAS

The simple conscious act of suspending our biases and acknowledging that we have a partial and incomplete view opens the door to productive dialogue.
November/December 2005

It has been said that dialogue evokes the best in people and draws forth commitment and enthusiasm; that occurs most effectively when there is a willingness to listen without judgment. So how do we open our minds to listen non-judgmentally?

We need to realize that the facts we gather and the assumptions we develop are always incomplete. They are only part of the story. It is as if we have only seen one part of a picture and have created a story—an understanding—built from that particular part.

We are meaning makers—given a small bit of information, we will interpret facts and amplify their meaning. Sometimes we are correct, but usually we are missing key pieces of information. We *think* we know, we *think* we have all the facts and know the whole story, but the story we know is the one we have fabricated from partial information.

We tend to pay attention to certain aspects of experience and to *not* notice others. Just as people witnessing an accident will have different versions of what happened, we create different interpretations from partial facts. The "facts" that we accumulate get incorporated into our underlying assumptions.

Yet, we don't have to be limited by our assumptions. By taking the time to suspend our biased interpretations and listen without judgment to another's, we open the way to a more complete understanding. We can acknowledge that we do not have all the facts and that our version of reality may be incomplete.

The simple conscious act of suspending our biases and acknowledging that we have a partial and incomplete view opens the door to productive dialogue. To fully tap the collective genius of a group, each individual's perspective must be valued and included as part of the whole.

Karin Rade

Wherever you would like to effect relevant change, simply have a look through the window of incongruities and ask: what is going on that seems like it should not be, or what is not going on that seems like it should?

January 2006

In identifying important windows of opportunity for purposeful change, the widely acclaimed teacher, writer and philosopher, Peter Drucker, has provided an invaluable roadmap.

In his seminal work, *Innovation and Entrepreneurship*, Drucker identified seven windows through which the most meaningful and relevant clues and cues appear—*unexpected events, incongruities, process needs, market structure, demographics, perception,* and *new knowledge/ technology.* Monitoring the operating environment through these seven windows captures the vital information that can generate invigorating change.

After the window of unexpected events, the window of *incongruities* usually produces the ripest opportunities for productive change. Incongruities are those events where something is happening that ought *not* be or when something is not happening that seems that it *should* be.

An example of an incongruity converted to productive innovation is the American Dream Project. The Corporation for Enterprise Development (CFED) created the project as an experi mental program to help break the cycle of poverty for the working poor.

The incongruity the project addresses is a fundamental social inequity: About 90% of the wealth generated in the United States is garnered by the wealthiest 20% of the population.

The American Dream Project created Individual Development Accounts (IDA)—savings accounts for the working poor. The program provides matching funds for investments in homes, business start-ups, and education. They also provide training for families in the essentials of personal finance.

Conceived in 1997 with just three local initiatives, the project grew by the year 2000 to include more than 225 initiatives serving over 5,000 account holders. In those three years the program generated more than $1.3 million in deposits. Their project demonstrates how incongruities can serve as catalysts for powerful and purposeful change.

Incongruities of various sorts are everywhere—in the organizations we serve, in our personal lives, and like this one, in the social infrastructure of our communities. Wherever you would like to effect relevant change, simply have a look through the window of incongruities and ask: what is going on that seems like it should not be, or what is *not* going on that seems like it should?

FAILURE: THE GREAT LEARNING OPPORTUNITY

Failure provides the vital learning that we need on the winding road to developing and implementing anything new.

February 2006

W e all fail. It is part of human nature. We create value from failures when we turn them into opportunities for learning.

The more we try something new or different, the more mistakes we will tend to make. It is virtually axiomatic that we will fail sometime, somewhere if we are pushing the envelope of possibility.

National Geographic photographer Dewitt Jones illustrates the point. For the typical National Geographic article, he takes thousands of pictures to get the few photographs needed for the article. The vast majority of his shots are never used—they are "failures." They were not good enough to make the final cut. The only way for him to stop failing is to stop taking pictures!

Oprah Winfrey, who has achieved astonishing renown and admiration, has a great attitude about failure. She said that she has never had any real failures—*only great learning opportunities.*

The phenomenally successful industrial design firm IDEO has adopted a business motto that has become a way of life for the firm: "Fail early to succeed sooner." They understand that failures are essential on the iterative journey to success.

In the early days of IBM, Tom Watson brought an executive into his office considered responsible for a failed project that had cost the company millions. The executive assumed he would be fired on the spot. But he wasn't. Watson told him that the company had just paid millions for his education; he was more valuable to the company now that he had *learned* from failing.

Failure. We may all be bit risk averse about failure. Early in our education, we may have acquired an aversion to the red-pencil F on our schoolwork. Bad. Dumb. Slow. Lacking. These were the early negative connotations of failure.

We need to see failure in a new and positive light. Failure provides the vital learning that we need on the winding road to developing and implementing anything new. Fail? Yes. Fail *early* so that we can succeed sooner!

Chris Stearns

SLOW COOK THE BIG INNOVATIONS

Little creative initiatives can and should happen quickly. Heat them in the microwave and go. But big changes need time. Slow cook them and you will serve up stronger social capital and creativity for the sustenance of the organization.

January 2007

We were delighted to see that January has been designated "International Creativity Month." Why the designation? "To remind individuals and organizations around the globe to capitalize on the power of creativity. Unleashing creativity and innovation is vital for personal and business success in this age of accelerating change."

Wait a minute. Someone must have been visiting our web site. We might as well end this month's essay right there. That is the whole point of everything we do.

Unleash creativity and innovation because it is vital for personal and organizational success in this age of accelerating change.

The end.

But wait. Did you know that January is also "National Slow Cooking Month?"

Neither did we.

It took over thirty years, since the slow cooker was introduced in 1970, to finally give that culinary innovation its own designated month of the year. They slow cooked it.

Innovation and slow cooking; there must be a connection there that transcends the month of the year they share. I have been slow cooking that possible connection all month. Then it hit me, like a flash fire:

Slow cook your *big* innovations.

What are the major innovations that you are contemplating for your organization—the ones that will impact everyone in the organization? Not the little ones that will only impact a few, the big ones that will affect everybody.

Slow cook them.

Big change needs some time to simmer. Through big changes, you will either build the social capital of the organization or deplete it. Creativity and social capital are directly correlated. If you deplete social capital, you deplete creativity.

Build social capital by enlisting the perspectives of many for the big innovations. Blend and simmer those perspectives until they congeal as a flavorful dish that people are eager to implement.

Then serve up a sample; don't serve the whole dish. Let people taste test it with some experience. Then simmer it some more.

Little creative initiatives can and should happen quickly. Heat them in the microwave and go. But big changes need time. Slow cook them and you will serve up stronger social capital *and* creativity for the sustenance of the organization.

*Organizational change happens
continuously in the simple conversations
that occur informally. This is where
shared stories provide the catalytic
impetus for change.*
June 2007

Compare the conversations in a formal meeting with a tight agenda to the "water-cooler" conversations you have informally with people, between the big meetings where the real "work" is being done. Which were more fruitful or insightful?

In our experience, the water-cooler conversations often produce the best stuff. Their informality allows for the free flow of conversation.

Informal conversations provide opportunities for *making sense* of information. They allow for a more spontaneous give and take—a flow of ideas and information that has a life of its own. Formal meetings can constrict that flow with tight agendas, political maneuvering, or expectations about behavioral norms.

The iterative nature of informal conversation is more conducive to producing insight and epiphany. They make sense of the here and now while shedding light on new possibilities.

Ideas, epiphanies, insights do not seem to proceed well along a tight agenda in a formal meeting. They are not subject to laws of linear cause and effect. They are born more spontaneously and unexpectedly.

Organizational change happens continuously in the simple conversations that occur informally. This is where shared stories provide the catalytic impetus for change. Simple conversations are not just *a medium for* change; they *create* change while they build social capital.

Informal conversations are indispensable to an innovative culture. There need to be plenty of places and times for people to talk freely, spontaneously, and informally.

Karin Rade

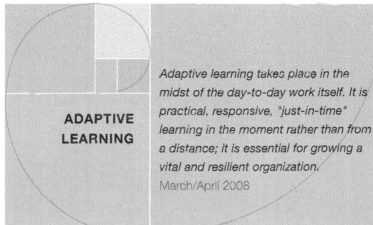

ADAPTIVE LEARNING

Adaptive learning takes place in the midst of the day-to-day work itself. It is practical, responsive, "just-in-time" learning in the moment rather than from a distance; it is essential for growing a vital and resilient organization.

March/April 2008

Adaptive learning takes place from day to day and moment to moment. It is practical "just-in-time" learning that is vital for organizations to thrive and prosper.

Strategic planning retreats are valuable opportunities to learn and share knowledge, to step back and see the big picture—the broad strategic view and the road ahead. *Adaptive learning* is where the rubber meets the road.

When Dwight Eisenhower said, "Plans are nothing; planning is everything," he was implicitly referring to the value of adaptive learning. Plans may look perfect in the boardroom, the retreat site, or the command center, but *implementing* plans requires perpetual improvisation and flexibility—*adaptive learning*.

The knowledge that shapes strategies is seldom fixed in stone; it is often dynamically unpredictable. The operating environment of any organization is understood from both the grandiose perspective of big-picture thinking and the particular experience, moment to moment, of the people doing the work.

The two, *together*, enable the organization to make productive and useful sense of experience and information.

For adaptive learning to be most effective, channels of communication must be fluid, egalitarian, and collaborative. Everyone—no matter what the job function—has a vital perspective to contribute. Everyone plays a role in co-creating the social and cultural fabric of organizational resilience.

Collaborative genius consists of the ongoing dialogue that occurs among people from all corners of the organization. Every problem becomes an opportunity to adapt more effectively. Every surprising piece of information becomes an opportunity to adjust to the new knowledge.

Adaptive learning takes place in the midst of the day-to-day work itself. It is practical, responsive, "just-in-time" learning *in the moment* rather than from a distance; it is essential for growing a vital and resilient organization.

Karin Rade

That is the fundamental formula for successful innovation anywhere in any industry or organization: learn, talk, create—the three strokes of the engine of innovation.

June 2008

Three words summarize the change we recommend for organizations: Learn * Talk * Create.

All of our training, our coaching, our facilitating, and our consulting concentrate on building the capacity of individuals to learn each of those three vital skills. When people in an organization freely engage those three fundamental phases of the creative cycle, they activate an engine of productive innovation that perpetually revitalizes the organization.

The cycle always begins with "learning." Without learning, creativity is subjective artistic expression. For creative thinking to be productively innovative, it must be based on learning.

In this month's letter, we offer an example of how simple, everyday learning—talked about and creatively acted upon—can dramatically transform an organization's operations.

The year was 1949. The fledgling Honda Motor Company made small, rugged 50cc motorized bikes for use in cities; it sold about 1200 per year in a decimated Japanese market. By 1959, they were selling 285,000 bikes and expanding.

After a careful assessment of the U.S. market and thorough strategic planning, they sent three employees to Los Angeles to introduce their new motorcycles designed to compete in the U.S. market. From their market research, Honda knew their small bikes would not sell in the U.S. Only larger, more powerful European and American road bikes sold here.

Their motorcycles designed for the U.S. market failed miserably. Frustrated, their three employees rode their small Honda-made 50cc bikes on weekends, in the hills surrounding L.A.

Locals started to take notice. It looked like fun. They purchased some of the bikes for themselves. Soon, others also clamored for the bikes. After a couple of years, the three employees woke up to the opportunity that had grown up around them. They convinced management that they had just found a new market niche in the U.S.—*recreational* bikes rather than heavy long-distance bikes.

It took some adjustments to their distribution and selling strategies; management had to be convinced to abandon their strategic plan, but the three were successful in launching the Honda 50cc Super Cub in the U.S. A UCLA marketing student came up with the slogan that would become a household phrase: "You meet the nicest people on a Honda." Sales exploded.

As Honda gained supremacy at the low end of the motorcycle market, they eventually turned their attention to the higher end. By 1975 they dominated the entire industry. Profits from motorized bikes were invested in manufacturing cars, where Honda would also make their mark.

In 2008, Honda announced that *sixty million* Super Cubs had been sold worldwide—the best selling motorized vehicle in history.

The story of Honda's success started with learning—paying attention to what was failing and what was succeeding, talking about it, and making innovative adjustments. That is the fundamental formula for successful innovation anywhere in any industry or organization: *learn, talk, create*—the three strokes of the engine of innovation.

THE FLOWER OF STRATEGIC INNOVATION

These are the game-changing moments when abrupt discontinuities rupture gaping fissures in the implicit rules and presumptions of economic enterprise.
Nov/Dec 2008

Credit has dried up; people are being laid off. Corporations are cutting back on production and services. Some, like the stalwarts GM and Ford, may declare bankruptcy. Wall Street has been decimated—some of the "masters of the universe" have been canned. The financial net worth of people around the world has plummeted.

These are the times that are ripe with opportunity.

These are the game-changing moments when abrupt discontinuities rupture gaping fissures in the implicit rules and presumptions of economic enterprise. Every new fissure is a window of opportunity—full of new light and nourishment—for the germinating flower of innovation.

These are the moments that innovators dream about—when all of the traditional operating norms and assumptions are challenged. Without shocking and anxious episodes like the one we are in, antiquated practices and outworn premises continue to govern business as usual.

This is clearly no longer business as usual.

Everything—from top to bottom—is in flux. The traditional jigsaw puzzle picture of normality has just been tossed in the air. A new puzzle picture is interactively in formation as pieces acquire new attributes creating a remodeled landscape.

Seldom do opportunities for innovation arrive in such abundance. These are not the simple innovations that are the stuff of day-to day operations. Those are *always* available.

This is a thunderstorm of wrenching discontinuities. These startling and abrupt continental shifts in the economic landscape seldom arrive with such devastating momentum. In a heavy storm, there may be much rain, but the flower of strategic innovation gets plenty of nourishment.

Where will the flowers of renewing strategic innovation most likely bloom? We will find them in changes in *market structures* and *changes in perception*.

This is a time that people in organizations everywhere should be pausing to evaluate their own strategic opportunities for change. These are the key questions to ask: What changes in *perception* or in *market structure* might we capitalize on as opportunities for strategic innovation?

Here are a few broad examples of the sort of answers those questions might elicit:

* General Motors, Lehman Brothers, AIG and other very big names have changed the perception that bigger is better and more secure.

* Smaller, tightly focused organizations will gain market footing.

* People will become more self-reliant and parsimonious.

+ Sovereign governments around the world have just taken a big step in the direction of global coordination.

+ Homeowners will think again about assuming that their house is an investment.

+ The assumption that top management knows best and deserves its unbalanced compensation has just been upended.

+ The luster of American financial stability has been badly tarnished.

+ Individuals and organizations will be less inclined to regard debt as a carbonated beverage.

What are the changes in perception or market structure that may touch your organization? Take some focused time to review them with others in your organization. The changes you notice constitute fissures in the hard rock of business-as-usual that have exposed fertile new soil for the flower of strategic innovation. Cultivate *that* soil and watch the flowers bloom.

Innovation: Follow Through

Capitalizing on Success

Change in organizations is often most easily accomplished by affirming what is already going well, and then doing more of it. You could use the space below to note the essays on innovation that highlight your current success and also what more you might do to build on that success.

Essay Title	What else could be done?

Fixing Problems

While affirming and capitalizing on success may be the easiest way to grow collaborative genius, problems may also have to be addressed. You could use the space below to note essays that have highlighted impediments to growing collaborative genius, and what you might do to address them.

Essay Title	What could be done?

Further Reading

These are among the books and articles that have helped to shape the work of Partners for Innovation. They have provided much of the intellectual foundation for "the art of of bringing organizations to life."

Bacik, James J. *Contemporary Theologians.* Fleming H. Revel, 1991

Belasco, James. *Teaching the Elephant to Dance: The Manager's Guide to Empowering Change.* Penguin, 1991.

Belasco, James and Stayer, Ralph C. Flight of the Buffalo: Soaring to Excellence, Learning to Let Employees Lead. Warner Books, Inc., 1994.

Bennis, Warren G. and Biederman, Patricia W. *Organizing Genius: The Secrets of Creative Collaboration.* Perseus Publishing, 1998.

Bolen, Jean Shinoda. *Gods in Every Man: A New Psychology of Men's Lives and Loves.* Harper Trade, 1990.

_____ __. *Goddesses in Every Woman: A New Psychology of Women.* HarperCollins Publishing, 1985.

Borg, Marcus. *Jesus and Buddha: The Parallel Sayings.* Ulysses Press, 1997

_____. *The God We Never Knew: Beyond Dogmatic Religion to a More Authentic Faith.* HarperSanFrancisco,1998.

Cameron, Julia. *The Artist's Way: A Spiritual Path to Higher Creativity.* J.P. Tarcher, 1992.

Campbell, Joseph. *The Hero With A Thousand Faces.* Princeton University Press, 1973.

Capra, Fritjof. *The Tao of Physics: An Exploration of the Parallels Between Modern Physics and Eastern Mysticism.* Shambhala Publications, Inc., 1999.

Christensen, Clayton. *The Innovator's Dilemma: When New Technologies Cause Great Firms to Fail.* Harvard Business School Publishing, 1997.

Collins, Jim *Good to Great: Why Some Companies Make the Leap... and Others Don't.* HarperCollins Publishers, 2001.

Collins, Jim and Porras, Jerry. *Built to Last: Successful Habits of Visionary Companies.* Harper Business, 1996.

Cooperrider, David L. et. al. eds. *Appreciative Inquiry: Rethinking Human Organization Toward Positive Theory of Change.* Stipes Publishing L.L.C., 1999.

Csikszentmilhalyi, Mihaly. *Creativity: Flow and the Psychology of Discovery and Invention.* HarperTrade, 1997.

Dannemiller Tyson Associates. *The Whole-Scale Change Toolkit.* Berrett-Koehler Publishers, 2000.

_____. *Whole-Scale Change, Unleashing the Magic in Organizations.* Berrett-Koehler Publishers, 2000.

De Bono, Edward. *de Bono's Thinking Course.* Facts on File, Inc., 1994.

De Geus, Arie. *The Living Company: Habits for Survival in a Turbulent Business.* Harvard Business School Publishing, 1997

Deming, W. Edwards. *Out of the Crisis.* MIT Press, 2000.

Drucker, Peter. *Innovation and Entrepreneurship: Practice and Principles.* Harper Business, 1986.

_____. *Management Challenges for the 21st Century.* Harper Business, 2001.

_____. *Managing in Turbulent Times*. Harper Business, 1985.

_____. *Managing in A Time of Great Change*. Dutton/Plume, 1997.

_____. *Managing for the Future: The 1990's and Beyond*. Plume/Penguin, 1993.

_____. *Managing for Results: Economic Tasks and Risk-Taking Decisions*. HarperInformation, 1986.

_____. *The Age of Discontinuity: Guidelines to Our Changing Society*. Transaction Publishers, 1992.

_____. *The New Realities: In Government and Politics, In Economics and Business, In Society and World View*. Harper Business, 1994.

Drucker, Peter with contributions by De Pree, Max and Buford, Robert. *Managing the Non-Profit Organization*. Harper Business, 1992.

Dyer, Wayne. *Your Sacred Self*. HarperCollins Publishers, 1996.

Emerson, Ralph Waldo; Atkinson, Brooks ed. *The Essential Writings of Ralph Waldo Emerson*. Random House Inc., 2000.

Estes, Clarissa Pinkola. *Women Who Run with the Wolves: Myths and Stories of the Wild Woman Archetype*. Ballantine Books, Inc., 1996.

Foster, Richard. *Innovation: The Attacker's Advantage*. Summit Books, 1986.

Fox, Matthew. *The Reinvention of Work: A New Vision of Livelihood for Our Time*. HarperCollins Publishers, Inc., 1995.

Fox, Matthew and Tucci, Candy. *Meditations with Meister Eckhart*. Bear & Company, 1984.

Hamel, Gary. *Leading the Revolution*. Harvard Business School Publishing, 2000.

Hamel, Gary and Phahalad, C.K. *Competing for the Future*. Harvard Business School Publishing, 1996.

Handy, Charles. The Age of Paradox. Harvard Business Press, 1995.

Hargrove, Robert and Senge, Peter. *Mastering the Art of Creative Collaboration*. McGraw-Hill Professional, 1997.

Hill, Napoleon. *Think and Grow Rich*. Ballentine Publishing Group, 1976.

Hillman, James. *The Soul's Code, In Search of Character and Calling*. Warner Books, 1997.

Hock, Dee. *Birth of the Chaordic Age*. Berrett-Koehler, 1999.

Hoenig, Christopher. *The Problem Solving Journey, Your Guide for Making Decisions and Getting Results*. Perseus Publishing, 2000.

Isaacs, William. *Dialogue and the Art of Thinking Together: A Pioneering Approach to Communicating in Business and in Life*. Doubleday & Company, Inc., 1999.

Jackson, Phil. *Sacred Hoops: Spiritual Lessons of a Hardwood Warrior*. Hyperion Press, 1996.

Jacobs, Jane. *The Death and Life of Great American Cities*. Random House, 1993.

Jacobsen, Mary-Elaine. *Liberating Everyday Creativity*. Ballantine Books, 1999.

James, William. *The Varieties of Religious Experience*. Modern Library 1994.

Jaworski, Joseph. *Synchronicity: The Inner Path of Leadership*. Berrett-Koehler Publishers, 1998.

Jung, C.G. *The Archetypes & the Collective Unconscious*. (CW 9). Princeton University Press, 1980.

_____. *Memories, Dreams, Reflections*. Vintage Books, 1989.

_____. *Modern Man in Search of a Soul*. Harcourt, 1976.

_____. *Psychological Reflections*. Princeton University Press, 1973.

_____. *Psychological Types*. (CW 6). Princeton University Press, 1976.

_____. *Synchronicity: An Acausal Connecting Principle*. Princeton University Press, 1972.

Kao, John. *Jamming: The Art and Discipline of Business Creativity*. Harper Business, 1997.

Katzenbach, Jon. *The Wisdom of Teams: Creating the High-Performance Organization*. Harper Business, 1994.

Kelly, Tom. *The Art of Innovation: Lessons in Creativity from IDEO, America's Leading Design Firm*. Doubleday & Company, Inc., 2001.

Kleiner, Art. *The Age of Heretics: Heroes, Outlaws, and the Forerunners of Corporate Change*. Bantam Doubleday Dell Publishing Group, 1996.

Levy, Steven. *Insanely Great: The Life and Times of the Macintosh, the Computer That Changed Everything*. Viking Penguin, 1993.

Liker, Jeffrey K. *The Toyota Way: 14 Management Principles from the World's Greatest Manufacturer*. McGraw-Hill, 2004.

Loomis, Mary E. *Dancing the Wheel of Psychological Types*. Chiron Publications, 1991.

Maslow, Abraham. *Maslow on Management*. John Wiley & Sons, 1998.

_____. *Toward a Psychology of Being*. Van Nostrand Reinhold, 1968.

Michalko, Michael. *Cracking Creativity: The Secrets of Creative Genius*. Ten Speed Press, 2001.

Mintzberg, Henry. *The Rise and Fall of Strategic Planning: Reconceiving Roles for Planning, Plans, Planners*. Simon & Shuster Trade, 1993.

Moore, Robert and Gillette, Douglas. *King, Warrior, Magician, Lover: Rediscovering the Archetypes of the Mature Masculine.* HarperCollins Publishers, Inc., 1991.

_____. *The King Within: Accessing the King in the Male Psyche.* William Morrow & Co., 1993.

Moore, Thomas. *Care of the Soul, a Guide for Cultivating Depth and Sacredness in Everyday Life.* HarperTrade, 1993.

Myers, Isabel Briggs. *Gifts Differing: Understanding Personality Type.* Consulting Psychologists Press, Inc., 1980.

Nesbitt, John. *Megatrends 2000: New Directions for Tomorrow.* William Morrow and Co., 1991.

O'Reilly, Charles III and Tushman, Michael. *Winning Through Innovation.* Harvard Business School Press, Revised Edition, 2002.

Patino, Rick. *Success is a Choice: Ten Steps to Overachieving in Business and Life.* Broadway Books, 1997.

Pearson, Carol. *The Hero Within.* Harper & Row, 1986.

Peck, M. Scott. *The Different Drum: Community Making and Peace.* Simon & Schuster, 1987.

_____. *The Road Less Traveled: A New Psychology of Love, Traditional Values and Spiritual Growth.* Simon and Schuster Trade, 1997.

Peters, Tom. *The Circle of Innovation: You Can't Shrink Your Way to Greatness.* Alfred A. Knopf, 1997.

_____. *The Pursuit of Wow: Every Person's Guide to Topsy-Turvy Times.* Random House, 1994.

Pfeffer, Jeffrey and Sutton, Robert I. *The Knowing-Doing Gap: How Smart Companies Turn Knowledge into Action.* Harvard Business School Publishing, 1999.

Phillips, Christopher. *Socrates Café.* W.W. Norton and Company, 2001.

Posner, Barry. *The Leadership Challenge*. Jossey-Bass, 2002.

Putnam, Robert D. *Bowling Alone*. Simon & Schuster, 2000.

Rhodes, Richard. *Making of the Atomic Bomb*. Simon & Schuster, 1995.

Rich, Ben. *Skunk Works*. Brown and Company, 1996.

Robbins, Harvey and Finley, Michael. *Why Teams Don't Work: What Went Wrong and How to Make it Right*. Peterson's, 1995.

Rogers, Everett M. *Diffusion of Innovation*. Simon & Schuster Trade, 1996.

Sanford, John. *The Kingdom Within: The Inner Meaning of Jesus' Sayings*. Harper San Francisco, 1987.

Schank, Roger and Childers, Peter G. *The Creative Attitude, Learning to Ask and Answer the Right Questions*. Macmillan Publishing Company, Inc., 1988.

Schumacher, E.F. *Small Is Beautiful: Economics as if People Mattered*. HarperTrade, 1989.

Seifter, Harvey. *Leadership Ensemble, Lessons in Collaborative Management from the World's Only Conductorless Orchestra*. Henry Holt & Company, Inc., 2001.

Semler, Ricardo. *Maverick: The Success Story Behind the World's Most Unusual Workplace*. Warner Books, Inc., 1994.

Senge, Peter, et. al. *The Dance of Change: The Challenges to Sustaining Momentum in a Learning Organization*. Doubleday & Company, Inc., 1999.

_____. *The Fifth Discipline: The Art and Practice of the Learning Organization*. Doubleday & Company, Inc., 1994.

Shrage, Michael. *Serious Play: How the World's Best Companies Simulate to Innovate*. Harvard Business School Publishing, 1999.

Smith, Douglas K. and Alexander, Robert C. *Fumbling the Future: How Xerox Invented, Then Ignored the First Personal Computer.* iUniverse.com, Inc., 1999.

Sobol, Robert. *When Giants Stumble: Classic Business Blunders and How to Avoid Them.* Prentice Hall Press, 1999.

Stack, Jack. *The Great Game of Business: Unlocking the Power and Profitability of Open-Book Management.* Doubleday & Company, 1994.

Thompson, D'Arcy. *On Growth and Form.* University of Cambridge, 1942, 1992.

Thoreau, Henry David. *Walden and Other Writings.* Barnes & Noble Books, 2000.

Toms, Michael and contributors. *The Soul of Business.* Hay House, Inc., 1997.

Townsend, Robert. *Further Up the Organization: How to Stop Management from Stifling People and Strangling Productivity.* Alfred Knopf, 1984.

Trout, Jack. *Differentiate or Die: Survival in Our Era of Killer Competition.* John Wiley and Sons, Inc., 2001.

Van Occh, Roger. *A Whack on the Side of the Head: How to Unlock Your Mind for Innovation.* Warner Books, 1983.

Von Frantz, Marie Louise and Hillman, James. *Jung's Typology.* Spring Publications, 1971.

Welch, Jack. *Jack: Straight from the Gut.* Warner Books, 2001.

Wheatley, Margaret. *Leadership and the New Science: Discovering Order in a Chaotic World.* Berrett-Koehler Publishers, 1999.

Wheatley, Margaret and Kellnor-Rogers, Myron. *A Simpler Way.* Berrett-Koehler Publishers, 1998.

Whyte, David. *The Heart Aroused: Poetry and the Preservation of the Soul in Corporate America*. Doubleday & Company, Inc., 1996.

Wills, Gary. *Papal Sin: Structures of Deceit*. Doubleday, 2000.

Wilson, Thomas B. *Innovative Reward Systems for the Changing Workplace*. McGraw-Hill Professional, 1994.

Zander, Rosamund and Zander, Benjamin. *The Art of Possibility: Transforming Professional and Personal Life*. Harvard Business School Publishing, 2000.

Articles

Amibile, Teresa. "How to Kill Creativity." *Harvard Business Review*. September-October, 1998.

Argyris, Chris. "Teaching Smart People How to Learn." *Harvard Business Review*. June, 2001.

Bellman, Matthias and Schaffer, Robert H. "Freeing Managers to Innovate." *Harvard Business Review*. June, 2001.

Bernick, Carol Levin. "When Your Culture Needs a Makeover." *Harvard Business Review*. June, 2001.

Bonabeau, Eric and Meyer, Christopher. "Swarm Intelligence: A Whole New Way to Think About Business." *Harvard Business Review*. May, 2001.

Case, John. "When Salaries Aren't Secret." *Harvard Business Review*. May, 2001.

Christiansen, Clayton M. "Assessing Your Organization's Innovative Capabilities." *Leader to Leader*. Vol 21, Summer, 2001.

Collins, Jim. "Turning Goals Into Results: The Power of Catalytic Mechanisms." *Harvard Business Review*. July-August, 1999.

Collins, James C. and Porras, Jerry I. "Building Your Company's Vision." *Harvard Business Review*. September-October, 1996.

Drucker, Peter. "The Discipline of Innovation." *Harvard Business Review*. November-December, 1998.

Eisenhardt, Kathleen and Sull, Donald N. "Strategy as Simple Rules." *Harvard Business Review*. January, 2001.

Hansen, Morten T. "Introducing T-shaped Managers: Knowledge Management's Next Generation." *Harvard Business Review*. March, 2001.

Leonard, Dorothy and Rayport, Jeffrey. "Spark Innovation Through Empathetic Design." *Harvard Business Review*. Nov-Dec, 1997.

Morgan, Nick. "How to Overcome 'Change Fatigue.'" *Harvard Management Update*. July, 2001.

Nemeth, Charlan Jeanne. "Managing Innovation: When Less is More." *California Management Review*. Vol 40, No. 1. Fall, 1997.

Oncken, William and Wass, Donald L. "Management Time: Who's Got the Monkey?" *Harvard Business Review*. November-December,1999.

Pfeffer, Jeffrey. "Six Dangerous Myths About Pay." *Harvard Business Review*. May-June, 1998.

Prokesch, Steven E. "Unleashing the Power of Learning: An Interview with British Petroleum's John Browne." *Harvard Business Review*. September-October, 1997.

Sandberg, Kirsten D. "The Case for Slack: Building 'Incubation Time' into Your Week." *Harvard Management Update*. June, 2001.

Seifter, Harvey. "The Conductor-less Orchestra." *Leader to Leader*. Vol. 21, Summer, 2001.

Semler, Ricardo. "How We Went Digital Without A Strategy." *Harvard Business Review*. Sept-Oct, 2000.

Sull, Donald N. "Why Good Companies Go Bad." *Harvard Business Review.* July-August, 1999.

Thomke, Stefan. "Enlightened Experimentation: The New Imperative for Innovation." *Harvard Business Review.* February, 2001.

Wetflaufer, Suzy. "The Business Case Against Revolution: An Interview with Nestle's Peter Brabeck." *Harvard Business Review.* February, 2001.

Zehnder, Egon. "A Simpler Way to Pay." Harvard Business Review. April, 2001.

About the Author

James Graham Johnston

Trained as an artist and an architect, schooled in business administration, and devoted to life-long learning in psychology, philosophy, and religion, James Johnston is an entrepreneur and author passionate about creating community and developing the unique potential of people.

He is co-founder of Partners for Innovation Inc. (www.partnersfi.com) the training company that helps grow the collaborative genius of people; founder of Gift Compass Inc. (www.GiftsCompass.com) the company that provides resources for living a uniquely authentic and fruitful life; and architect of the GiftsCompass Inventory, an online self-assessment that provides a compass for personal individuation.

He is the author of *The Call Within*, a guide to finding and following inner spiritual guidance, and the editor of "Innovation Tips"—the essays that comprise the content of this book.